Data Mining Models

Data Mining Models

Second Edition

David L. Olson

 BUSINESS EXPERT PRESS

Data Mining Models, Second Edition

First published in 2016 by
Business Expert Press, LLC
222 East 46th Street, New York, NY 10017
www.businessexpertpress.com

ISBN-13: 978-1-94858-049-6 (paperback)
ISBN-13: 978-1-94858-050-2 (e-book)

Business Expert Press Big Data and Business Analytics Collection

Collection ISSN: 2333-6749 (print)
Collection ISSN: 2333-6757 (electronic)

Cover and interior design by Exeter Premedia Services Private Ltd., Chennai, India

Second edition: 2018

10 9 8 7 6 5 4 3 2 1

Printed in the United States of America.

Abstract

Data mining has become the fastest growing topic of interest in business programs in the past decade. This book is intended to first describe the benefits of data mining in business, describe the process and typical business applications, describe the workings of basic data mining models, and demonstrate each with widely available free software. This second edition updates Chapter 1, and adds more details on Rattle data mining tools.

The book focuses on demonstrating common business data mining applications. It provides exposure to the data mining process, to include problem identification, data management, and available modeling tools. The book takes the approach of demonstrating typical business data sets with open source software. KNIME is a very easy-to-use tool, and is used as the primary means of demonstration. R is much more powerful and is a commercially viable data mining tool. We will demonstrate use of R through Rattle. We also demonstrate WEKA, which is a highly useful academic software, although it is difficult to manipulate test sets and new cases, making it problematic for commercial use. We will demonstrate methods with a small but typical business dataset. We use a larger (but still small) realistic business dataset for Chapter 9.

Keywords

big data, business analytics, clustering, data mining, decision trees, neural network models, regression models

Contents

Acknowledgments

I wish to recognize some of the many colleagues I have worked and published with, specifically Yong Shi, Dursun Delen, Desheng Wu, and Ozgur Araz. There are many others I have learned from in joint efforts as well, both students and colleagues, all of whom I wish to recognize with hearty thanks.

CHAPTER 1

Data Mining in Business

Introduction

Data mining refers to the analysis of large quantities of data that are stored in computers. Bar coding has made checkout very convenient for us and provides retail establishments with masses of data. Grocery stores and other retail stores are able to quickly process our purchases and use computers to accurately determine the product prices. These same computers can help the stores with their inventory management, by instantaneously determining the quantity of items of each product on hand. Computers allow the store's accounting system to more accurately measure costs and determine the profit that store stockholders are concerned about. All of this information is available based on the bar coding information attached to each product. Along with many other sources of information, information gathered through bar coding can be used for data mining analysis.

The era of big data is here, with many sources pointing out that more data are created over the past year or two than was generated throughout all prior human history. Big data involves datasets so large that traditional data analytic methods no longer work due to data volume. Davenport[1] gave the following features of big data:

- Data too big to fit on a single server
- Data too unstructured to fit in a row-and-column database
- Data flowing too continuously to fit into a static data warehouse
- Lack of structure is the most important aspect (even more than the size)
- The point is to *analyze*, converting data into insights, innovation, and business value

Big data has been said to be more about analytics than about the data itself. The era of big data is expected to emphasize focusing on knowing what (based on correlation) rather than the traditional obsession for causality. The emphasis will be on discovering patterns offering novel and useful insights.[2] Data will become a raw material for business, a vital economic input and source of value. Cukier and Mayer–Scheonberger[3] cite big data providing the following impacts on the statistical body of theory established in the 20th century: (1) There is so much data available that sampling is usually not needed (n = all). (2) Precise accuracy of data is, thus, less important as inevitable errors are compensated for by the mass of data (any one observation is flooded by others). (3) Correlation is more important than causality—most data mining applications involving big data are interested in what is going to happen, and you don't need to know why. Automatic trading programs need to detect the trend changes, not figure out that the Greek economy collapsed or the Chinese government will devalue the Renminbi (RMB). The programs in vehicles need to detect that an axle bearing is getting hot and the vehicle is vibrating and the wheel should be replaced, not whether this is due to a bearing failure or a housing rusting out.

There are many sources of big data.[4] Internal to the corporation, e-mails, blogs, enterprise systems, and automation lead to structured, unstructured, and semistructured information within the organization. External data is also widely available, much of it free over the Internet, but much also available from the commercial vendors. There also is data obtainable from social media.

Data mining is not limited to business. Both major parties in the U.S. elections utilize data mining of potential voters.[5] Data mining has been heavily used in the medical field, from diagnosis of patient records to help identify the best practices.[6] Business use of data mining is also impressive. Toyota used data mining of its data warehouse to determine more efficient transportation routes, reducing the time to deliver cars to their customers by an average 19 days. Data warehouses are very large scale database systems capable of systematically storing all transactional data generated by a business organization, such as Walmart. Toyota also was able to identify the sales trends faster and to identify best locations for new dealerships.

Data mining is widely used by banking firms in soliciting credit card customers, by insurance and telecommunication companies in detecting fraud, by manufacturing firms in quality control, and many other appli-cations. Data mining is being applied to improve food product safety, criminal detection, and tourism. *Micromarketing* targets small groups of highly responsive customers. Data on consumer and lifestyle data is widely available, enabling customized individual marketing campaigns. This is enabled by *customer profiling*, identifying those subsets of customers most likely to be profitable to the business, as well as *targeting*, determining the characteristics of the most profitable customers.

Data mining involves statistical and artificial intelligence (AI) analysis, usually applied to large-scale datasets. There are two general types of data mining studies. *Hypothesis testing* involves expressing a theory about the relationship between actions and outcomes. This approach is referred to as *supervised*. In a simple form, it can be hypothesized that advertising will yield greater profit. This relationship has long been studied by retailing firms in the context of their specific operations. Data mining is applied to identifying relationships based on large quantities of data, which could include testing the response rates to various types of advertising on the sales and profitability of specific product lines. However, there is more to data mining than the technical tools used. The second form of data min-ing study is *knowledge discovery*. Data mining involves a spirit of knowl-edge discovery (learning new and useful things). Knowledge discovery is referred to as *unsupervised*. In this form of analysis, a preconceived notion may not be present, but rather relationships can be identified by looking at the data. This may be supported by visualization tools, which display data, or through fundamental statistical analysis, such as correlation anal-ysis. Much of this can be accomplished through automatic means, as we will see in decision tree analysis, for example. But data mining is not limited to automated analysis. Knowledge discovery by humans can be enhanced by graphical tools and identification of unexpected patterns through a combination of human and computer interaction.

Requirements for Data Mining

Data mining requires identification of a problem, along with the collec-tion of data that can lead to better understanding, and computer models to provide statistical or other means of analysis. A variety of analytic computer models have been used in data mining. In the later sections, we will discuss various types of these models. Also required is access to data. Quite often, systems including data warehouses and data marts are used to manage large quantities of data. Other data mining analyses are done with smaller sets of data, such as can be organized in online analytic processing systems.

Masses of data generated from cash registers, scanning, and topic-specific databases throughout the company are explored, analyzed, reduced, and reused. Searches are performed across different models proposed for predicting sales, marketing response, and profit. The classical statistical approaches are fundamental to data mining. Automated AI methods are also used. However, a systematic exploration through classical statistical methods is still the basis of data mining. Some of the tools developed by the field of statistical analysis are harnessed through automatic control (with some key human guidance) in dealing with data.

Data mining tools need to be versatile, scalable, capable of accurately predicting the responses between actions and results, and capable of automatic implementation. *Versatile* refers to the ability of the tool to apply a wide variety of models. *Scalable* tools imply that if the tools works on a small dataset, it should also work on a larger dataset. Automation is useful, but its application is relative. Some analytic functions are often automated, but human setup prior to implementing procedures is required. In fact, analyst judgment is critical to successful implementation of data mining. Proper selection of data to include in searches is critical. Data transformation also is often required. Too many variables produce too much output, while too few can overlook the key relationships in the data.

Data mining is expanding rapidly, with many benefits to business. Two of the most profitable application areas have been the use of customer segmentation by marketing organizations to identify those with marginally greater probabilities of responding to different forms of marketing media, and banks using data mining to more accurately predict the likelihood of people to respond to the offers of different services offered. Many companies are using this technology to identify their blue-chip customers, so that they can provide them with the service needed to retain them.

The casino business has also adopted data warehousing and data mining. Historically, casinos have wanted to know everything about their customers. A typical application for a casino is to issue special cards, which are used whenever the customer plays at the casino, or eats, or stays, or spends money in other ways. The points accumulated can be used for complimentary meals and lodging. More points are awarded for activities that provide Harrah's more profit. The information obtained is sent to the firm's corporate database, where it is retained for several years. Instead of advertising the loosest slots in town, Bellagio and Mandalay Bay have developed the strategy of promoting luxury visits. Data mining is used to identify high rollers, so that these valued customers can be cultivated. Data warehouses enable casinos to estimate the lifetime value of the players. Incentive travel programs, in-house promotions, corporate business, and customer follow-up are the tools used to maintain the most profitable customers. Casino gaming is one of the richest datasets available. Very specific individual profiles can be developed. Some customers are identified as those who should be encouraged to play longer. Other customers are identified as those who are discouraged from playing.

Business Data Mining

Data mining has been very effective in many business venues. The key is to find *actionable* information or information that can be utilized in a concrete way to improve profitability. Some of the earliest applications were in retailing, especially in the form of market basket analysis. Table 1.1 shows the general application areas we will be discussing. Note that they are meant to be representative rather than comprehensive.

Table 1.1 Data mining application areas

Application area	Applications	Specifics
Retailing	Affinity positioning Cross-selling; develop and maintain customer loyalty	Position products effectively Find more products for customers
Banking	Customer relationship management (CRM)	Identify customer value Develop programs to maximize the revenue
Credit card management	Lift Churn (Loyalty)	Identify effective market segments Identify likely customer turnover

(Continued)

Table 1.1 Data mining application areas (Continued)

Application area	Applications	Specifics
Insurance	Fraud detection	Identify claims meriting investigation
Telecommunications	Churn	Identify likely customer turnover
Telemarketing	Online information Recommender systems	Aid telemarketers with easy data access
Human resource management	Churn (Retention)	Identify potential employee turnover

Retailing

Data mining offers retailers, in general, and grocery stores, specifically, valuable predictive information from mountains of data. Affinity positioning is based on the identification of products that the same customer is likely to want. For instance, if you are interested in cold medicine, you probably are interested in tissues. Thus, it would make marketing sense to locate both items within easy reach of the other. Cross-selling is a related concept. The knowledge of products that go together can be used by marketing the complementary product. Grocery stores do that through position product shelf location. Retail stores relying on advertising can send ads for sales on shirts and ties to those who have recently purchased suits. These strategies have long been employed by wise retailers. Recommender systems are effectively used by Amazon and other online retailers. Data mining provides the ability to identify less expected product affinities and cross-selling opportunities. These actions develop and maintain customer loyalty.

Grocery stores generate mountains of cash register data that require automated tools for analysis. Software is marketed to service a spectrum of users. In the past, it was assumed that cash register data was so massive that it couldn't be quickly analyzed. However, the current technology enables the grocers to look at customers who have defected from a store, their purchase history, and characteristics of other potential defectors.

Banking

The banking industry was one of the first users of data mining. Banks are turning to technology to find out what motivates their customers and what will keep their business (*customer relationship management*—CRM). CRM involves the application of technology to monitor customer service, a function that is enhanced through data mining support. Understanding the value a customer provides the firm makes it possible to rationally evaluate if extra expenditure is appropriate in order to keep the customer. There are many opportunities for data mining in banking. Data mining applications in finance include predicting the prices of equities involve a dynamic environment with surprise information, some of which might be inaccurate and some of which might be too complex to comprehend and reconcile with intuition.

Data mining provides a way for banks to identify patterns. This is valuable in assessing loan applications as well as in target marketing. Credit unions use data mining to track member profitability as well as monitoring the effectiveness of marketing programs and sales representatives. They also are used in the effort of member care, seeking to identify what credit union customers want in the way of services.

Credit Card Management

The credit card industry has proven very profitable. It has attracted many card issuers, and many customers carry four or five cards. Balance surfing is a common practice, where the card user pays an old balance with a new card. These are not considered attractive customers, and one of the uses of data warehousing and data mining is to identify balance surfers. The profitability of the industry has also attracted those who wish to push the edge of credit risk, both from the customer and the card issuer perspective. Bank credit card marketing promotions typically generate 1,000 responses to mailed solicitations, a response rate of about 1 percent. This rate is improved significantly through data mining analysis.

Data mining tools used by banks include credit scoring. Credit scoring is a quantified analysis of credit applicants with respect to the prediction of on-time loan repayment. A key is a consolidated data warehouse, covering all products, including demand deposits, savings, loans, credit cards, insurance, annuities, retirement programs, securities underwriting, and every other product banks provide. Credit scoring provides a number for each applicant by multiplying a set of weighted numbers determined by the data mining analysis multiplied times ratings for that applicant. These credit scores can be used to make accept or reject recommendations, as well as to establish the size of a credit line. Credit scoring used to be conducted by bank loan officers, who considered a few tested variables, such as employment, income, age, assets, debt, and loan history. Data mining makes it possible to include many more variables, with greater accuracy.

The new wave of technology is broadening the application of database use and targeted marketing strategies. In the early 1990s, nearly all credit card issuers were mass-marketing to expand their card-holder bases. However, with so many cards available, broad-based marketing campaigns have not been as effective as they initially were. Card issuers are more carefully examining the expected net present value of each customer. Data warehouses provide the information, giving the issuers the ability to try to more accurately predict what the customer is interested in, as well as their potential value to the issuer. Desktop campaign management software is used by the more advanced credit card issuers, utilizing data mining tools, such as neural networks, to recognize customer behavior patterns to predict their future relationship with the bank.

Insurance

The insurance industry utilizes data mining for marketing, just as retailing and banking organizations do. But, they also have specialty applications. Farmers Insurance Group has developed a system for underwriting, which generates millions of dollars in higher revenues and lower claims. The system allows the firm to better understand narrow market niches and to predict losses for specific lines of insurance. One discovery was that it could lower its rates on sports cars, which increased their market share for this product line significantly.

Unfortunately, our complex society leads to some inappropriate business operations, including insurance fraud. Specialists in this underground industry often use multiple personas to bilk insurance companies, especially in the automobile insurance environment. Fraud detection software use a similarity search engine, analyzing information in company claims for similarities. By linking names, telephone numbers, streets, birthdays, and other information with slight variations, patterns can be identified, indicating a fraud. The similarity search engine has been found to be able to identify up to seven times more fraud than the exact-match systems.

Telecommunications

Deregulation of the telephone industry has led to widespread competition. Telephone service carriers fight hard for customers. The problem is that once a customer is obtained, it is attacked by competitors, and retention of customers is very difficult. The phenomenon of a customer switching carriers is referred to as *churn*, a fundamental concept in telemarketing as well as in other fields.

A director of product marketing for a communications company considered that one-third of churn is due to poor call quality and up to one-half is due to poor equipment. That firm has a wireless telephone performance monitor tracking telephones with poor performances. This system reduced churn by an estimated 61 percent, amounting to about 3 percent of the firm's overall subscribers over the course of a year. When a telephone begins to go bad, the telemarketing personnel are alerted to contact the customer and suggest bringing in the equipment for service.

Another way to reduce churn is to protect customers from subscription and cloning fraud. Cloning has been estimated to have cost the wireless industry millions. A number of fraud prevention systems are marketed. These systems provide verification that is transparent to the legitimate subscribers. Subscription fraud has been estimated to have an economic impact of $1.1 billion. Deadbeat accounts and service shutoffs are used to screen potentially fraudulent applicants.

Churn is a concept that is used by many retail marketing operations. Banks widely use churn information to drive their promotions. Once data mining identifies customers by characteristic, direct mailing and telemarketing are used to present the bank's promotional program. The mortgage market has seen massive refinancing in a number of periods. Banks were quick to recognize that they needed to keep their mortgage customers happy if they wanted to retain their business. This has led to banks contacting the current customers if those customers hold a mortgage at a rate significantly above the market rate. While they may cut their own lucrative financial packages, banks realize that if they don't offer a better service to borrowers, a competitor will.

Human Resource Management

Business intelligence is a way to truly understand markets, competitors, and processes. Software technology such as data warehouses, data marts, online analytical processing (OLAP), and data mining make it possible to sift through data in order to spot trends and patterns that can be used by the firm to improve profitability. In the human resources field, this analysis can lead to the identification of individuals who are liable to leave the company unless additional compensation or benefits are provided.

Data mining can be used to expand upon things that are already known. A firm might know that 20 percent of its employees use 80 percent of services offered, but may not know which particular individuals are in that 20 percent. Business intelligence provides a means of identifying segments, so that programs can be devised to cut costs and increase productivity. Data mining can also be used to examine the way in which an organization uses its people. The question might be whether the most talented people are working for those business units with the highest priority or where they will have the greatest impact on profit.

Companies are seeking to stay in business with fewer people. Sound human resource management would identify the right people, so that organizations could treat them well to retain them (reduce churn). This requires tracking key performance indicators and gathering data on talents, company needs, and competitor requirements.

Summary

The era of big data is here, flooding businesses with numbers, text, and often more complex data forms, such as videos or pictures. Some of this data is generated internally, through enterprise systems or other software tools to manage a business's information. Data mining provides a tool to utilize this data. This chapter reviewed the basic applications of data mining in business, to include customer profiling, fraud detection, and churn analysis. These will all be explored in greater depth in Chapter 2. But, here our intent is to provide an overview of what data mining is useful for in business.

The process of data mining relies heavily on information technology, in the form of data storage support (data warehouses, data marts, or OLAP tools) as well as software to analyze the data (data mining software). However, the process of data mining is far more than simply applying these data mining software tools to a firm's data. Intelligence is required on the part of the analyst in selection of model types, in selection and transformation of the data relating to the specific problem, and in interpreting results.

CHAPTER 2

Business Data Mining Tools

Have you ever wondered why your spouse gets all of these strange catalogs for obscure products in the mail? Have you also wondered at his or her strong interest in these things, and thought that the spouse was overly responsive to advertising of this sort? For that matter, have you ever wondered why 90 percent of your telephone calls, especially during meals, are opportunities to purchase products? (Or for that matter, why calls assuming you are a certain type of customer occur over and over, even though you continue to tell them that their database is wrong?)

One of the earliest and most effective business applications of data mining is in support of customer segmentation. This insidious application utilizes massive databases (obtained from a variety of sources) to segment the market into categories, which are studied with data mining tools to predict the response to particular advertising campaigns. It has proven highly effective. It also represents the probabilistic nature of data mining, in that it is not perfect. The idea is to send catalogs to (or call) a group of target customers with a 5 percent probability of purchase rather than waste these expensive marketing resources on customers with a 0.05 percent probability of purchase. The same principle has been used in election campaigns by party organizations—give free rides to the voting booth to those in your party; minimize giving free rides to voting booths to those likely to vote for your opponents. Some call this bias. Others call it sound business.

Data mining offers the opportunity to apply technology to improve many aspects of business. Some standard applications are presented in this chapter. The value of education is to present you with past applications, so that you can use your imagination to extend these application ideas to new environments.

Data mining has proven valuable in almost every academic discipline. Understanding business application of data mining is necessary to expose business college students to current analytic information technology. Data mining has been instrumental in customer relationship management,[1] credit card management,[2] banking,[3] insurance,[4] telecommunications,[5] and many other areas of statistical support to business. Business data mining is made possible by the generation of masses of data from computer information systems. Understanding this information generation system and tools available leading to analysis is fundamental for business students in the 21st century. There are many highly useful applications in practically every field of scientific study. Data mining support is required to make sense of the masses of business data generated by computer technology.

This chapter will describe some of the major applications of data mining. By doing so, there will also be opportunities to demonstrate some of the different techniques that have proven useful. Table 2.1 compares the aspects of these applications.

A wide variety of business functions are supported by data mining. Those applications listed in Table 2.1 represent only some of these applications. The underlying statistical techniques are relatively simple—to predict, to identify the case closest to past instances, or to identify some pattern.

Table 2.1 Common business data mining applications

Application	Function	Statistical technique	AI tool
Catalog sales	Customer segmentation Mail stream optimization	Cluster analysis	K-means Neural network
CRM (telecom)	Customer scoring Churn analysis	Cluster analysis	Neural network
Credit scoring	Loan applications	Cluster analysis Pattern search	K-means
Banking (loans)	Bankruptcy prediction	Prediction Discriminant analysis	Decision tree
Investment risk	Risk prediction	Prediction	Neural network
Insurance	Customer retention (churn) Pricing	Prediction Logistic regression	Decision tree Neural network

Customer Profiling

We begin with probably the most spectacular example of business data mining. Fingerhut, Inc. was a pioneer in developing methods to improve business. In this case, they sought to identify the small subset of the most likely purchasers of their specialty catalogs. They were so successful that they were purchased by Federated Stores. Ultimately, Fingerhut operations were a victim to the general malaise in IT business in 2001 and 2002. But, they still represent a pioneering development of data mining application in business.

Lift

This section demonstrates the concept of lift used in customer segmentation models. We can divide the data into groups as fine as we want (here, we divide them into 10 equal portions of the population, or groups of 10 percent each). These groups have some identifiable features, such as zip code, income level, and so on (a profile). We can then sample and identify the portion of sales for each group. The idea behind lift is to send promotional material (which has a unit cost) to those groups that have the greatest probability of positive response first. We can visualize lift by plotting the responses against the proportion of the total population of potential customers, as shown in Table 2.2. Note that the segments are listed in Table 2.2 sorted by expected customer response.

Table 2.2 Lift calculation

Ordered segment	Expected customer response	Proportion (expected responses)	Cumulative response proportion	Random average proportion	Lift
Origin	0	0	0	0	0
1	0.20	0.172	0.172	0.10	0.072
2	0.17	0.147	0.319	0.20	0.119
3	0.15	0.129	0.448	0.30	0.148
4	0.13	0.112	0.560	0.40	0.160
5	0.12	0.103	0.664	0.50	0.164

(Continued)

Table 2.2 Lift calculation (Continued)

Ordered segment	Expected customer response	Proportion (expected responses)	Cumulative response proportion	Random average proportion	Lift
6	0.10	0.086	0.750	0.60	0.150
7	0.09	0.078	0.828	0.70	0.128
8	0.08	0.069	0.897	0.80	0.097
9	0.07	0.060	0.957	0.90	0.057
10	0.05	0.043	1.000	1.00	0.000

LIFT

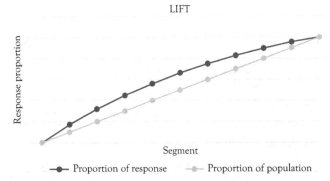

Figure 2.1 Lift identified by the mail optimization system

Both the cumulative responses and cumulative proportion of the population are graphed to identify the lift. Lift is the difference between the two lines in Figure 2.1.

The purpose of lift analysis is to identify the most responsive segments. Here, the greatest lift is obtained from the first five segments. We are probably more interested in profit, however. We can identify the most profitable policy. What needs to be done is to identify the portion of the population to send promotional materials to. For instance, if an average profit of $200 is expected for each positive response and a cost of $25 is expected for each set of promotional material sent out, it obviously would be more profitable to send to the first segment containing an expected 0.2 positive responses ($200 times 0.2 equals an expected revenue of $40, covering the cost of $25 plus an extra $15 profit). But, it still might be possible to improve the overall profit by sending to other segments as well (always selecting the segment with the larger response rates in order). The plot of cumulative profit is shown in Figure 2.2 for this set of data. The second most responsive segment would also be profitable, collecting $200 times 0.17 or $34 per $25 mailing for a net profit of $9. It turns out that the fourth most responsive segment collects 0.13 times $200 ($26) for a net profit of $1, while the fifth most responsive segment collects $200 times 0.12 ($24) for a net loss of $1. Table 2.3 shows the calculation of the expected payoff.

The profit function in Figure 2.2 reaches its maximum with the fourth segment.

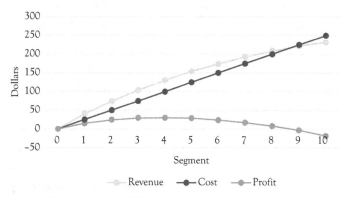

Figure 2.2 Profit impact of lift

Table 2.3 Calculation of the expected payoff

Segment	Expected segment revenue ($200 × P)	Cumulative expected revenue	Random cumulative cost ($25 × i)	Expected payoff
0	0	0	0	0
1	40	40	25	15
2	34	74	50	24
3	30	104	75	29
4	26	130	100	30
5	24	154	125	29
6	20	174	150	24
7	18	192	175	17
8	16	208	200	8
9	14	222	225	-3
10	10	232	250	-18

It is clear that the maximum profit is found by sending to the four most responsive segments of the ten in the population. The implication is that in this case, the promotional materials should be sent to the four segments expected to have the largest response rates. If there was a promotional budget, it would be applied to as many segments as the budget would support, in order of the expected response rate, up to the fourth segment.

It is possible to focus on the wrong measure. The basic objective of lift analysis in marketing is to identify those customers whose decisions will be influenced by marketing in a positive way. In short, the methodology described earlier identifies those segments of the customer base that would be expected to purchase. This may or may not have been due to the marketing campaign effort. The same methodology can be applied, but more detailed data is needed to identify those whose decisions would have been changed by the marketing campaign, rather than simply those who would purchase.

Another method that considers multiple factors is Recency, Frequency, and Monetary (RFM) analysis. As with lift analysis, the purpose of an RFM is to identify customers who are more likely to respond to new offers. While lift looks at the static measure of response to a particular campaign, RFM keeps track of customer transactions by time, by frequency, and by amount. Time is important as some customers may not have responded to the last campaign, but might now be ready to purchase the product being marketed. Customers can also be sorted by the frequency of responses and by the dollar amount of sales. The subjects are coded on each of the three dimensions (one approach is to have five cells for each of the three measures, yielding a total of 125 combinations, each of which can be associated with a positive response to the marketing campaign). The RFM still has limitations, in that there are usually more than three attributes important to a successful marketing program, such as product variation, customer age, customer income, customer lifestyle, and so on.[6] The approach is the basis for a continuing stream of techniques to improve customer segmentation marketing.

Understanding lift enables understanding the value of specific types of customers. This enables more intelligent customer management, which is discussed in the next section.

Comparisons of Data Mining Methods

Initial analyses focus on discovering patterns in the data. The classical statistical methods, such as correlation analysis, is a good start, often supplemented with visual tools to see the distributions and relationships among variables. Clustering and pattern search are typically the first activities in data analysis, good examples of *knowledge discovery*. Then, appropriate models are built. Data mining can then involve model building (extension of the conventional statistical model building to very large datasets) and pattern recognition. Pattern recognition aims to identify groups of interesting observations. Often, experts are used to assist in pattern recognition.

There are two broad categories of models used for data mining. Continuous, especially time series, data often calls for forecasting. Linear regression provides one tool, but there are many others. Business data mining has widely been used for classification or developing models to predict which category a new case will most likely belong to (such as a customer profile relative to the expected purchases, whether or not loans will be problematic, or whether insurance claims will turn out to be fraudulent). The classification modeling tools include statistically based logistic regression as well as artificial intelligence-based neural networks and decision trees.

Sung et al. compared a number of these methods with respect to their advantages and disadvantages. Table 2.4 draws upon their analysis and expands it to include the other techniques covered.

Knowledge Discovery

Clustering: One unsupervised clustering technique is partitioning, the process of examining a set of data to define a new categorical variable partitioning the space into a fixed number of regions. This amounts to dividing the data into clusters. The most widely known partitioning algorithm is k-means, where k center points are defined, and each observation is classified to the closest of these center points. The k-means algorithm attempts to position the centers to minimize the sum of distances. Centroids are used as centers, and the most commonly used distance metric is

Table 2.4 *Comparison of data mining method features*[7]

Method	Advantages	Disadvantages	Assumptions
Cluster analysis	Can generate understandable formula Can be applied automatically	Computation time increases with dataset size Requires identification of parameters, with results sensitive to choices	Need to make data numerical
Discriminant analysis	Ability to incorporate multiple financial ratios simultaneously Coefficients for combining the independent variables Ability to apply to new data	Violates normality and independence assumptions Reduction of dimensionality issues Varied interpretation of the relative importance of variables Difficulty in specifying the classification algorithm Difficulty in interpreting the time-series prediction tests	Assume multivariate normality within groups Assume equal group covariances across all groups Groups are discrete, nonoverlapping, and identifiable
Regression	Can generate understandable formula Widely understood Strong body of theory	Computation time increases with dataset size Not very good with nonlinear data	Normality of errors No error autocorrelation, heteroskedasticity, multicollinearity

Neural network models	Can deal with a wide range of problems Produce good results in complicated domains (nonlinear) Can deal with both continuous and categorical variables Have many software packages available	Require inputs in the range of 0 to 1 Do not explain results May prematurely converge to an inferior solution	Groups are discrete, nonoverlapping, and identifiable
Decision trees	Can generate understandable rules Can classify with minimal computation Use easy calculations Can deal with continuous and categorical variables Provide a clear indication of variable importance	Some algorithms can only deal with binary-valued target classes Most algorithms only examine a single field at a time Can be computationally expensive	Groups are discrete, nonoverlapping, and identifiable

Euclidean. Instead of k-means, k-median can be used, providing a partitioning method expected to be more stable.

Pattern search: Objects are often grouped to seek patterns. Clusters of customers might be identified with particularly interesting average outcomes. On the positive side, you might look for patterns in highly profitable customers. On the negative side, you might seek patterns unique to those who fail to pay their bills to the firm.

Both clustering and pattern search seek to group the objects. Cluster analysis is attractive, in that it can be applied automatically (although ample computational time needs to be available). It can be applied to all types of data, as demonstrated in our example. Cluster analysis is also easy to apply. However, its use requires selection from among alternative distance measures, and weights may be needed to reflect variable importance. The results are sensitive to these measures. Cluster analysis is appropriate when dealing with large, complex datasets with many variables and specifically identifiable outcomes. It is often used as an initial form of analysis. Once different clusters are identified, pattern search methods are often used to discover the rules and patterns. Discriminant analysis has been the most widely used data mining technique in bankruptcy prediction. Clustering partitions the entire data sample, assigning each observation to exactly one group. Pattern search seeks to identify local clusterings, in that there are more objects with similar characteristics than one would expect. Pattern search does not partition the entire dataset, but identifies a few groups exhibiting unusual behavior. In the application on real data, clustering is useful for describing broad behavioral classes of customers. Pattern search is useful for identifying groups of people behaving in an anomalous way.

Predictive Models

Regression is probably the most widely used analytical tool historically. A main benefit of regression is the broad understanding people have about regression models and tests of their output. Logistic regression is highly appropriate in data mining, due to the categorical nature of resultant variables that is usually present. While regression is an excellent tool for statistical analysis, it does require assumptions about parameters. Errors are assumed to be normally distributed, without autocorrelation (errors are not related to the prior errors), without heteroskedasticity (errors don't grow with time, for instance), and without multicollinearity (independent variables don't contain high degrees of overlapping information content). Regression can deal with nonlinear data, but only if the modeler understands the underlying nonlinearity and develops appropriate variable transformations. There usually is a tradeoff—if the data are fit well with a linear model, regression tends to be better than neural network models. However, if there is nonlinearity or complexity in the data, neural networks (and often, genetic algorithms) tend to do better than regression. A major relative advantage of regression relative to neural networks is that regression provides an easily understood formula, while neural network models have a very complex model.

Neural network algorithms can prove highly accurate, but involve difficulty in the application to new data or interpretation of the model. Neural networks work well unless there are many input features. The presence of many features makes it difficult for the network to find patterns, resulting in long training phases, with lower probabilities of convergence. Genetic algorithms have also been applied to data mining, usually to bolster operations of other algorithms.

Decision tree analysis requires only the last assumption, that groups are discrete, nonoverlapping, and identifiable. They provide the ability to generate understandable rules, can perform classification with minimal computation, and these calculations are easy. Decision tree analysis can deal with both continuous and categorical variables, and provide a clear indication of variable importance in prediction and classification. Given the disadvantages of the decision tree method, it is a good choice when the data mining task is classification of records or prediction of outcomes.

Summary

Data mining applications are widespread. This chapter sought to give concrete examples of some of the major business applications of data mining. We began with a review of Fingerhut data mining to support catalog sales. That application was an excellent demonstration of the concept of lift applied to retail business. We also reviewed five other major business applications, intentionally trying to demonstrate a variety of different functions, statistical techniques, and data mining methods. Most of those studies applied multiple algorithms (data mining methods). Software such as Enterprise Miner has a variety of algorithms available, encouraging data miners to find the method that works best for a specific set of data.

The second portion of the book seeks to demonstrate these methods with small demonstration examples. The small examples can be run on Excel or other simple spreadsheet packages with statistical support. Businesses can often conduct data mining without purchasing large-scale data mining software. Therefore, our philosophy is that it is useful to understand what the methods are doing, which also provides the users with better understanding of what they are doing when applying data mining.

CHAPTER 3

Data Mining Processes and Knowledge Discovery

In order to conduct data mining analysis, a general process is useful. This chapter describes an industry standard process, which is often used, and a shorter vendor process. While each step is not needed in every analysis, this process provides a good coverage of the steps needed, starting with data exploration, data collection, data processing, analysis, inferences drawn, and implementation.

There are two standard processes for data mining that have been presented. CRISP-DM (cross-industry standard process for data mining) is an industry standard, and SEMMA (sample, explore, modify, model, and assess) was developed by the SAS Institute Inc., a leading vendor of data mining software (and a premier statistical software vendor). Table 3.1 gives a brief description of the phases of each process. You can see that they are basically similar, only with different emphases.

Industry surveys indicate that CRISP-DM is used by over 70 percent of the industry professionals, while about half of these professionals use their own methodologies. SEMMA has a lower reported usage, as per the KDNuggets.com survey.

Table 3.1 CRISP-DM and SEMMA

CRISP-DM	SEMMA
Business understanding	Assumes well-defined questions
Data understanding	Sample
Data preparation	Explore
Modeling	Modify data
Evaluation	Model
Deployment	Assess

CRISP-DM

CRISP-DM is widely used by the industry members. This model consists of six phases intended as a cyclical process shown in Figure 3.1.

This six-phase process is not a rigid, by-the-numbers procedure. There is usually a great deal of backtracking. Additionally, experienced analysts may not need to apply each phase for every study. But, CRISP-DM provides a useful framework for data mining.

Business Understanding

The key element of a data mining study is understanding the purpose of the study. This begins with the managerial need for new knowledge and the expression of the business objective of the study to be undertaken. Goals in terms of things, such as which types of customers are interested in each of our products or what are the typical profiles of our customers, and how much value do each of them provide to us, are needed. Then, a plan for finding such knowledge needs to be developed, in terms of those responsible for collecting data, analyzing data, and reporting. At this stage, a budget to support the study should be established, at least in preliminary terms.

Data Understanding

Once the business objectives and the project plan are established, data understanding considers data requirements. This step can include initial

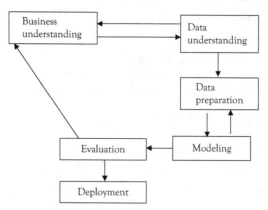

Figure 3.1 CRISP-DM process

data collection, data description, data exploration, and verification of data quality. Data exploration, such as viewing summary statistics (which includes visual display of the categorical variables), can occur at the end of this phase. Models such as cluster analysis can also be applied during this phase, with the intent of identifying patterns in the data.

Data sources for data selection can vary. Normally, the types of data sources for business applications include *demographic data* (such as income, education, number of households, and age), *sociographic data* (such as hobby, club membership, and entertainment), *transactional data* (sales record, credit card spending, and issued checks), and so on. The data type can be categorized as quantitative and qualitative data. *Quantitative data* is measurable by numerical values. It can be either discrete (such as integers) or continuous (such as real numbers). *Qualitative data*, also known as categorical data, contains both nominal and ordinal data. Nominal data has finite nonordered values, such as gender data having two values: male and female. Ordinal data has finite ordered values. For example, customer credit ratings are ordinal data since ratings can be excellent, fair, or bad.

Data Preparation

The purpose of data preprocessing is to clean the selected data for better quality. Some selected data may have different formats because they are chosen from different data sources. If selected data are from flat files, voice messages, and web texts, they should be converted to a consistent electronic format. In general, data cleaning means to filter, aggregate, and fill the missing values (*imputation*). By filtering data, the selected data are examined for outliers and redundancies. Outliers have huge differences from the majority of data or data that are clearly out of range of the selected data groups. For example, if the income of a customer included in the middle class is $250,000, it is an error and should be taken out from the data mining project examining aspects of the middle class. Outliers may be caused by many reasons, such as human errors or technical errors, or may naturally occur in a dataset due to extreme events. Suppose the age of a credit card holder is recorded as 12. This is likely a human error. However, there may be such an independently wealthy preteenager with important purchasing habits. Arbitrarily deleting this outlier could lose valuable information.

Redundant data are the same information recorded in several different ways. The daily sales of a particular product are redundant to seasonal sales of the same product, because we can derive the sales from either daily data or seasonal data. By aggregating data, the data dimensions are reduced to obtain aggregated information. Note that although an aggregated dataset has a small volume, the information will remain. If a marketing promotion for furniture sales is considered in the next three or four years, then the available daily sales data can be aggregated as annual sales data. The size of the sales data is dramatically reduced. By smoothing data, the missing values of the selected data are found and new or reasonable values will be added. These added values could be the average number of the variable (mean) or the mode. A missing value often causes no solution when a data mining algorithm is applied to discover the knowledge patterns.

Data can be expressed in a number of different forms. For instance, in CLEMENTINE, the following data types can be used:

- RANGE: numeric values (integer, real, or date and time).
- FLAG: binary—yes or no, 0 or 1, or other data with two outcomes—(text, integer, real number, or date and time).
- SET: data with distinct multiple values (numeric, string, or date and time).
- TYPELESS: for other types of data.

Usually, we think of data as real numbers, such as age in years or annual income in dollars (we would use RANGE in those cases). Sometimes, variables occur as either and or types, such as having a driving license or not, an insurance claim being fraudulent or not. This case could be dealt with by real numeric values (such as 0 or 1). But, it is more efficient to treat them as FLAG variables. Often it is more appropriate to deal with categorical data, such as age in terms of the set {young, middle-aged, elderly} or income in the set {low, middle, high}. In that case, we could group the data and assign the appropriate category in terms of a string, using a set. The most complete form is RANGE, but sometimes data does not come in that form, and analysts are forced to use SET or FLAG types.

Sometimes, it may actually be more accurate to deal with SET data types than RANGE data types.

As another example, PolyAnalyst (a typical treatment) has the following data types available:

- numerical   continuous values
- integer   integer values
- yes or no   binary data
- category   a finite set of possible values
- date
- string
- text

Each software tool will have a different data scheme, but the primary types of data dealt with are represented in these two lists.

There are many statistical methods and visualization tools that can be used to preprocess the selected data. Common statistics, such as max, min, mean, and mode, can be readily used to aggregate or smooth the data, while scatter plots and box plots are usually used to filter outliers. More advanced techniques, including regression analysis, cluster analysis, decision tree, or hierarchical analysis, may be applied in data preprocessing depending on the requirements for the quality of the selected data. Because data preprocessing is detailed and tedious, it demands a great deal of time. In some cases, data preprocessing could take over 50 percent of the time of the entire data mining process. Shortening data processing time can reduce much of the total computation time in data mining. The simple and standard data format resulting from data preprocessing can provide an environment of information sharing across different computer systems, which creates the flexibility to implement various data mining algorithms or tools.

Modeling

Data modeling is where the data mining software is used to generate results for various situations. Cluster analysis and or visual exploration of the data is usually applied first. Depending on the type of data, various models might then be applied. If the task is to group data and the groups are given, discriminant analysis might be appropriate. If the purpose is estimation, regression is appropriate if the data is continuous (and logistic regression, if not). Neural networks could be applied for both tasks. Decision trees are yet another tool to classify data. Other modeling tools are available as well. The point of data mining software is to allow the user to work with the data to gain understanding. This is often fostered by the iterative use of multiple models.

Data treatment: Data mining is essentially analysis of the statistical data, usually using very large datasets. The standard process of data mining is to take this large set of data and divide it using a portion of the data (the *training set*) for the development of the model (no matter which modeling technique is used), and reserving a portion of the data (the *test set*) for testing the model that is built. The principle is that if you build a model on a particular set of data, it will of course test quite well. By dividing the data and using part of it for model development, and testing it on a separate set of data, a more convincing test of model accuracy is obtained.

This idea of splitting the data into components is often carried to the additional levels in the practice of data mining. Further portions of the data can be used for refinement of the model.

Data mining techniques: Data mining can be achieved by association, classification, clustering, predictions, sequential patterns, and similar time sequences.

In *association*, the relationship of some item in a data transaction with other items in the same transaction is used to predict patterns. For example, if a customer purchases a laptop PC (X), then he or she also buys a mouse (Y) in 60 percent of the cases. This pattern occurs in 5.6 percent of laptop PC purchases. An association rule in this situation can be "X implies Y, where 60 percent is the confidence factor and 5.6 percent is the support factor." When the confidence factor and support factor are represented by linguistic variables "high" and "low," respectively, the association rule can be written in the fuzzy logic form, such as "when the support factor is low, X implies Y is high." In the case of many qualitative variables, fuzzy association is a necessary and promising technique in data mining.

Sequential pattern analysis seeks to find similar patterns in data transaction over a business period. These patterns can be used by the business analysts to identify relationships among data. The mathematical models behind sequential patterns are logic rules, fuzzy logic, and so on. As an extension of sequential patterns, *similar time sequences* are applied to discover sequences similar to a known sequence over the past and current business periods. In the data mining stage, several similar sequences can be studied to identify the future trends in transaction development. This approach is useful in dealing with databases that have time-series characteristics.

We have already discussed the important tools of clustering, prediction, and classification in Chapter 2.

Evaluation

The data interpretation stage is very critical. It assimilates knowledge from mined data. There are two essential issues. One is how to recognize the business value from knowledge patterns discovered in the data mining stage. Another issue is which visualization tool should be used to show the data mining results. Determining the business value from discovered knowledge patterns is similar to playing "puzzles." The mined data is a puzzle that needs to be put together for a business purpose. This operation depends on the interaction between data analysts, business analysts, and decision makers (such as managers or CEOs). Because data analysts may not be fully aware of the purpose of the data mining goal or objective, while business analysts may not understand the results of sophisticated mathematical solutions, interaction between them is necessary. In order to properly interpret knowledge patterns, it is necessary to choose an appropriate visualization tool. There are many visualization packages or tools available, including pie charts, histograms, box plots, scatter plots, and distributions. A good interpretation will lead to productive business decisions, while a poor interpretation analysis may miss useful information. Normally, the simpler the graphical interpretation, the easier it is for the end users to understand.

Deployment

Deployment is the act of using data mining analyses. New knowledge generated by the study needs to be related to the original project goals.

Once developed, models need to be monitored for performance. The patterns and relationships developed based on the training set need to be changed if the underlying conditions generating the data change. For instance, if the customer profile performance changes due to the changes in the economic conditions, the predicted rates of response cannot be expected to remain the same. Thus, it is important to check the relative accuracy of data mining models and adjust them to new conditions, if necessary.

SEMMA

In order to be applied successfully, the data mining solution must be viewed as a process, rather than a set of tools or techniques. In addition to the CRISP-DM, there is yet another well-known methodology developed by the SAS Institute Inc., called SEMMA. The acronym SEMMA stands for sample, explore, modify, model, and assess. Beginning with a statistically representative sample of your data, SEMMA intends to make it easy to apply the exploratory statistical and visualization techniques, select and transform the most significant predictive variables, model the variables to predict outcomes, and finally, confirm a model's accuracy.

By assessing the outcome of each stage in the SEMMA process, one can determine how to model new questions raised by the previous results, and thus, proceed back to the exploration phase for additional refinement of the data. That is, as is the case with CRISP-DM, SEMMA is also driven by a highly iterative experimentation cycle.

Step 1 (Sample)

This is where a portion of a large dataset (big enough to contain the significant information, yet small enough to manipulate quickly) is extracted. For optimal cost and computational performance, some (including the SAS Institute Inc.) advocate a sampling strategy, which applies a reliable, statistically representative sample of the full-detail data. In the case of very large datasets, mining a representative sample instead of the whole volume may drastically reduce the processing time required to get crucial business information. If general patterns appear in the data as a whole, these will be traceable in a representative sample. If a niche (a rare pattern) is so tiny that it is not represented in a sample and yet so important that it influences the big picture, then it should be discovered using the exploratory data description methods. It is also advised to create partitioned datasets for better accuracy assessment.

- Training—used for model fitting.
- Validation—used for assessment and for preventing over fitting.
- Test—used to obtain an honest assessment of how well a model generalizes.

A more detailed discussion and relevant techniques for the assessment and validation of data mining models is given in Chapter 5 of this book.

Step 2 (Explore)

This is where the user searches for unanticipated trends and anomalies in order to gain a better understanding of the dataset. After sampling your data, the next step is to explore them visually or numerically for inherent trends or groupings. Exploration helps refine and redirect the discovery process. If visual exploration does not reveal clear trends, one can explore the data through statistical techniques, including factor analysis, correspondence analysis, and clustering. For example, in data mining for a direct mail campaign, clustering might reveal the groups of customers with distinct ordering patterns. Limiting the discovery process to each of these distinct groups individually may increase the likelihood of exploring richer patterns that may not be strong enough to be detected if the whole dataset is to be processed together.

Step 3 (Modify)

This is where the user creates, selects, and transforms the variables upon which to focus the model-construction process. Based on the discoveries in the exploration phase, one may need to manipulate data to include information, such as the grouping of customers and significant subgroups, or to introduce new variables. It may also be necessary to look for outliers and reduce the number of variables, to narrow them down to the most significant ones. One may also need to modify data when the "mined" data change. Because data mining is a dynamic, iterative process, you can update the data mining methods or models when new information is available.

Step 4 (Model)

This is where the user searches for a variable combination that reliably predicts a desired outcome. Once you prepare your data, you are ready to construct models that explain patterns in the data. Modeling techniques in data mining include artificial neural networks, decision trees, rough set analysis, support vector machines, logistic models, and other statistical models, such as time-series analysis, memory-based reasoning, and principal component analysis. Each type of model has particular strengths and is appropriate within the specific data mining situations, depending on the data. For example, artificial neural networks are very good at fitting highly complex nonlinear relationships, while rough sets analysis is known to produce reliable results with uncertain and imprecise problem situations.

Step 5 (Assess)

This is where the user evaluates the usefulness and reliability of the findings from the data mining process. In this final step of the data mining process, the user assesses the models to estimate how well it performs. A common means of assessing a model is to apply it to a portion of dataset put aside (and not used during the model building) during the sampling stage. If the model is valid, it should work for this reserved sample as well as for the sample used to construct the model. Similarly, you can test the model against known data. For example, if you know which customers in a file had high retention rates and your model predicts retention, you can check to see whether the model selects these customers accurately. In addition, practical applications of the model, such as partial mailings in a direct mail campaign, help prove its validity.

The SEMMA approach is completely compatible with the CRISP-DM approach. Both aid the knowledge discovery process. Once the models are obtained and tested, they can then be deployed to gain value with respect to a business or research application.

Evaluation of Model Results

We demonstrate with a dataset divided into a training set (about two-thirds of 2,066 cases) and test set (the remaining cases). Datasets are sometimes divided into three (or may be more) groups if a lot of model development is conducted. The basic idea is to develop models on the training set and then test the resulting models on the test set. It is typical to try to develop multiple models (such as various decision trees, logistic regression, and neural network models) for the same training set and to evaluate errors on the test set.

Classification errors are commonly displayed in *coincidence matrixes* (called confusion matrixes by some). A coincidence matrix shows the count of cases correctly classified as well as the count of cases classified in each incorrect category. But, in many data mining studies, the model may be very good at classifying one category, while very poor at classifying another category. The primary value of the coincidence matrix is that it identifies what kinds of errors are made. It may be much more important to avoid one kind of error than another. Assume a loan vice president suffers a great deal more from giving a loan to someone who's expected to repay and does not, than making the mistake of not giving a loan to an applicant who actually would have paid. Both instances would be classification errors, but in data mining, often one category of error is much more important than another. Coincidence matrixes provide a means of focusing on what kinds of errors particular models tend to make.

When classifying data, in the simplest binary case, there are two opportunities for the model to be wrong. If the model is seeking to predict true or false, correctly classifying true is *true positive* (TP), and correctly classifying false is *true negative* (TN). One type of error is to incorrectly classify an actual false as true (*false positive* (FP), *type I error*). A second type of error is to incorrectly classify an actual true case as false (*false negative* (FN), *type II error*).

A way to reflect the relative error importance is through cost. This is a relatively simple idea, allowing the user to assign relative costs by the type of error. For instance, if our model predicted that an account was insolvent, that might involve an average write-off of $500. On the other hand, waiting for an account that ultimately was repaid might involve a cost of $20. Thus, there would be a major difference in the cost of errors in this case. Treating a case that turned out to be repaid as a dead account would risk the loss of $480 in addition to alienating the customer (which may or may not have future profitability implications). Conversely, treating an account that was never going to be repaid may involve carrying the account on the books longer than needed, at an additional cost of $20. Here, a cost function for the coincidence matrix could be:

$500 × (closing good account) + $20 × (keeping bad account open)

(Note that we used our own dollar costs for purposes of demonstration and were not based on the real case.) This measure (like the correct classification rate) can be used to compare alternative models. We assume a model is built on a training set (predicting 250 defaults), which is then applied to a test set of 1,000 cases (200 of which defaulted and 800 paid back, or were OK). The coincidence matrix for this model is displayed in Table 3.2.

The overall classification accuracy is obtained by dividing the correct number of classifications (150 + 700 = 850) by the total number of cases (1,000). Thus, the test data was correctly classified in 0.85 of the cases. The cost function value here was:

$500 × 50 + $20 × 100 = $27,000

Table 3.2 The coincidence matrix—equal misclassification costs

Loans	Model default	Model OK	
Actual default	150	50	200
Actual OK	100	700	800
	250	750	1,000

There are a number of other measures obtainable from the confusion matrix. Most are self-defining, such as:

True positive rate (TPR), which is equal to TP/(TP + FN) (also called *sensitivity*)

True negative rate (TNR) equal to TN/(FP + TN) (also called *specificity*)

Positive predictive value (PPV) equal to TP/(TP + FP) (also called *precision*)

Negative predictive value (NPV) equal to TN/(TN + FN)

False positive rate (FPR) equal to FP/(FP + TN) (also called *fall-out*)

False discovery rate (FDR) equal to FP/(FP + TP)

False negative rate (FNR) equal to FN/FN + TP) (also called *miss rate*).

Accuracy is equal to (TP + TN)/(TP + TN + FP + FN)

A *receiver operating characteristic* (ROC) curve is obtained by plotting TPR versus FPR for various threshold settings. This is equivalent to plotting the cumulative distribution function of the detection probability on the y axis versus the cumulative distribution of the false-alarm probability on the x axis.

Summary

The industry standard CRISP-DM process has six stages: (1) business understanding, (2) data understanding, (3) data preparation, (4) modeling, (5) evaluation, and (6) deployment. SEMMA is another process outline with a very similar structure. Using the CRISP-DM framework, data selection and understanding, preparation, and model interpretation require teamwork between data mining analysts and business analysts, while data transformation and data mining are conducted by data mining analysts. Each stage is a preparation for the next stage. In the remainder chapters of this book, we will discuss the details of this process from a different perspective, such as data mining tools and applications. This will provide the reader with a better understanding on why the correct process, sometimes, is even more important than correct performance of the methodology.

CHAPTER 4

Overview of Data Mining Techniques

Data useful to business comes in many forms. For instance, an automobile insurance company, faced with millions of accident claims, realizes that not all claims are legitimate. If they are extremely tough and investigate each claim thoroughly, they will spend more money on investigation than they would pay in claims. They also will find that they are unable to sell new policies. If they are as understanding and trusting as their television ads imply, they will reduce their investigation costs to zero, but will leave themselves vulnerable to fraudulent claims. Insurance firms have developed ways to profile claims, considering many variables, to provide an early indication of cases that probably merit expending funds for investigation. This has the effect of reducing the overall policy expenses, because it discourages fraud, while minimizing the imposition on valid claims. The same approach is used by the Internal Revenue Service in processing individual tax returns. Fraud detection has become a viable data mining industry, with a large number of software vendors. This is typical of many applications of data mining.

Data mining can be conducted in many business contexts. This chapter presents four datasets that will be utilized to demonstrate the techniques to be covered in Part II of the book. In addition to insurance fraud, files have been generated reflecting other common business applications, such as loan evaluation and customer segmentation. The same concepts can be applied to other applications, such as evaluation of the employees.

We have described data mining, its process, and data storage systems that make it possible. The next section of the book will describe the data mining methods. Data mining tools have been classified by the tasks of classification, estimation, clustering, and summarization. Classification and estimation are predictive. Clustering and summarization are descriptive. Not all methods will be presented, but those most commonly used will be. We will demonstrate each of these methods with small example datasets intended to show how these methods work. We do not intend to give the impression that these datasets are anywhere near the scale of real data mining applications. But, they do represent the micro versions of real applications and are much more convenient to demonstrate concepts.

Data Mining Models

Data mining uses a variety of modeling tools for a variety of purposes. Various authors have viewed these purposes along with the available tools (see Table 4.1). These methods come from both classical statistics as well as from artificial intelligence. Statistical techniques have strong diagnostic tools that can be used for the development of confidence intervals on parameter estimates, hypothesis testing, and other things. Artificial intelligence techniques require fewer assumptions about the data and are generally more automatic.

Table 4.1 Data mining modeling tools

Algorithms	Functions	Basis	Task
Cluster detection	Cluster analysis	Statistics	Classification
Regression	Linear regression	Statistics	Prediction
	Logistic regression	Statistics	Classification
	Discriminant analysis	Statistics	Classification
Neural networks	Neural networks	AI	Classification
	Kohonen nets	AI	Cluster
Decision trees	Association rules	AI	Classification
Rule induction	Association rules	AI	Description
Link analysis			Description
	Query tools		Description
	Descriptive statistics	Statistics	Description
	Visualization tools	Statistics	Description

Regression comes in a variety of forms, to include ordinary least squares regression, logistic regression (widely used in data mining when outcomes are binary), and discriminant analysis (used when outcomes are categorical and predetermined).

The point of data mining is to have a variety of tools available to assist the analyst and user in better understanding what the data consists of. Each method does something different, and usually, this implies a specific problem is best treated with a particular algorithm type. However, sometimes different algorithm types can be used for the same problem. Most involve setting the parameters, which can be important in the effectiveness of the method is needed. Further, the output needs to be interpreted.

There are a number of overlaps. Cluster analysis helps data miners to visualize the relationship among customer purchases, and is supported by visualization techniques that provide a different perspective. Link analysis helps identify the connections between variables, often displayed through graphs as a means of visualization. An example of link analysis application is in telephony, where calls are represented by the linkage between the caller and the receiver. Another example of linkage is the physician referral patterns. A patient may visit their regular doctor, who detects something that they don't know a lot about. They refer to their network of acquaintances to identify a reliable specialist who does. Clinics are collections of physician specialists, and might be referred to for especially difficult cases.

Data Mining Perspectives

Methods can be viewed from different perspectives. From the perspective of statistics and operations research, data mining methods include:

- Cluster analysis
- Regression of various forms
- Discriminant analysis (use of linear regression for classification)
- Line fitting through the operations research tool of multiple objective linear programming

From the perspective of artificial intelligence, these methods include:

- Neural networks (best fit methods)
- Rule induction (decision trees)
- Genetic algorithms (often used to supplement other methods)

Regression and neural network approaches are best fit methods and are usually applied together. Regression tends to have advantages with linear data, while neural network models do very well with irregular data. Software usually allows the user to apply variants of each and lets the analyst select the model that fits best. Cluster analysis, discriminant analysis, and case-based reasoning seek to assign new cases to the closest cluster of past observations. Rule induction is the basis of decision tree methods of data mining. Genetic algorithms apply to the special forms of data and are often used to boost or improve the operation of other techniques.

The ability of some of these techniques to deal with the common data mining characteristics is compared in Table 4.2.

Table 4.2 demonstrates that there are different tools for different types of problems. If the data is especially noisy, this can lead to difficulties for

Table 4.2 General ability of data mining techniques to deal with data features

Data characteristic	Rule induction	Neural networks	Case-based reasoning	Genetic algorithms
Handle noisy data	Good	Very good	Good	Very good
Handle missing data	Good	Good	Very good	Good
Process large datasets	Very good	Poor	Good	Good
Process different data types	Good	Transform to numerical	Very good	Transformation needed
Predictive accuracy	High	Very high	High	High
Explanation capability	Very good	Poor	Very good	Good
Ease of integration	Good	Good	Good	Very good
Ease of operation	Easy	Difficult	Easy	Difficult

the classical statistical methods, such as regression, cluster analysis, and discriminant analysis. The methods using rule induction and case-based reasoning can deal with such problems, but if the noise was false information, this can lead to rules concluding the wrong things. Neural networks and genetic algorithms have proven useful relative to the classical methods in environments where there are complexities in the data, to include interactions among variables that are nonlinear.

Neural networks have relative disadvantages in dealing with very large numbers of variables, as the computational complexity increases dramatically. Genetic algorithms require a specific data structure for genetic algorithms to operate, and it is not always easy to transform data to accommodate this requirement.

Another negative feature of neural networks is their hidden nature. Due to the large number of node connections, it is impractical to print out and analyze a large neural network model. This makes it difficult to transport a model built on one system to another system. Therefore, new data must be entered in the system where the neural network model was built in order to apply it to the new cases. This makes it nearly impossible to apply neural network models outside of the system upon which they are built.

Data Mining Functions

Problem types can be described in four categories:

- *Association* identifies the rules that determine the relationships among entities, such as in market basket analysis, or the association of symptoms with diseases.
- *Prediction* identifies the key attributes from data to develop a formula for prediction of future cases, as in regression models.
- *Classification* uses a training dataset to identify classes or clusters, which then are used to categorize data. Typical applications include categorizing risk and return characteristics of investments and credit risk of loan applicants.
- *Detection* determines the anomalies and irregularities, valuable in fraud detection.

Table 4.3 compares the common techniques and applications by business area.

Table 4.3 Data mining applications by method

Area	Technique	Application	Problem type
Finance	Neural network	Forecast stock price	Prediction
	Neural network	Forecast bankruptcy	Prediction
	Rule induction	Forecast price index futures	Prediction
		Fraud detection	Detection
	Neural network	Forecast interest rates	Prediction
	Case-based reasoning		
	Neural network	Delinquent bank loan detection	Detection
	Visualization		
	Rule induction	Forecast defaulting loans	Prediction
		Credit assessment	Prediction
		Portfolio management	Prediction
		Risk classification	Classification
		Financial customer classification	Classification
	Rule induction	Corporate bond rating	Prediction
	Case-based reasoning		
	Rule induction	Loan approval	Prediction
	Visualization		
Telecom	Neural network	Forecast network behavior	Prediction
	Rule induction		
	Rule induction	Churn management	Classification
		Fraud detection	Detection
	Case-based reasoning	Call tracking	Classification
Marketing	Rule induction	Market segmentation	Classification
		Cross-selling improvement	Association
	Rule induction	Lifestyle behavior analysis	Classification
	Visualization	Product performance analysis	Association
	Rule induction	Customer reaction to promotion	Prediction
	Genetic algorithm		
	Visualization		
	Case-based reasoning	Online sales support	Classification

Web	Rule induction Visualization	User browsing similarity analysis	Classification, Association
	Rule-based heuristics	Web page content similarity	Association
Others	Neural network	Software cost estimation	Detection
	Neural network Rule induction	Litigation assessment	Prediction
	Rule induction	Insurance fraud detection Healthcare exception reporting	Detection Detection
	Case-based reasoning	Insurance claim estimation Software quality control	Prediction Classification
	Genetic algorithms	Budget expenditure	Classification

Many of these applications combined techniques to include visualization and statistical analysis. The point is that there are many data mining tools available for a variety of functional purposes, spanning almost every area of human endeavor (including business). This section of the book seeks to demonstrate how these primary data mining tools work.

Demonstration Datasets

We will use some simple models to demonstrate the concepts. These datasets were generated by the authors, reflecting important business applications. The first model includes loan applicants, with 20 observations for building data, and 10 applicants serving as a test dataset. The second dataset represents job applicants. Here, 10 observations with known outcomes serve as the training set, with 5 additional cases in the test set. A third dataset of insurance claims has 10 known outcomes for training and 5 observations in the test set. All three datasets will be applied to new cases.

Larger datasets for each of these three cases will be provided as well as a dataset on expenditure data. These larger datasets will be used in various chapters to demonstrate methods.

Loan Analysis Data

This dataset (Table 4.4) consists of information on applicants for appliance loans. The full dataset involves 650 past observations. Applicant information on age, income, assets, debts, and credit rating (from a credit bureau, with red for bad credit, yellow for some credit problems, and green for clean credit record) is assumed available from loan applications. Variable Want is the amount requested in the appliance loan application. For past observations, variable On-time is 1 if all payments were received on time and 0 if not (Late or Default). The majority of past loans were paid on time. Data was transformed to obtain categorical data for some of the techniques. Age was grouped by less than 30 (young), 60 or over (old), and in between (middle-aged). Income was grouped as less than or equal to $30,000 per year or lower (low income), $80,000 per year or more (high income), and average in between. Asset, debt, and loan amount (variable Want) are used by rule to generate categorical variable Risk. Risk was categorized as High if debts exceeded the assets, as low if assets exceeded the sum of debts plus the borrowing amount requested, and average in between.

Table 4.5 gives a test set of data.

The model can be applied to the new applicants given in Table 4.6.

Job Application Data

The second dataset involves 500 past job applicants. Variables are:

Age	integer, 20 to 65	
State	State of origin	
Degree	Cert	Professional certification
	UG	Undergraduate degree
	MBA	Masters in Business Administration
	MS	Masters of Science
	PhD	Doctorate
Major	none	
	Engr	Engineering
	Sci	Science or Math
	Csci	Computer Science

Table 4.4 Loan analysis training dataset

Age	Income	Assets	Debts	Want	Risk	Credit	Result
20 (young)	17,152 (low)	11,090	20,455	400	High	Green	On-time
23 (young)	25,862 (low)	24,756	30,083	2,300	High	Green	On-time
28 (young)	26,169 (low)	47,355	49,341	3,100	High	Yellow	Late
23 (young)	21,117 (low)	21,242	30,278	300	High	Red	Default
22 (young)	7,127 (low)	23,903	17,231	900	Low	Yellow	On-time
26 (young)	42,083 (average)	35,726	41,421	300	High	Red	Late
24 (young)	55,557 (average)	27,040	48,191	1,500	High	Green	On-time
27 (young)	34,843 (average)	0	21,031	2,100	High	Red	On-time
29 (young)	74,295 (average)	88,827	100,599	100	High	Yellow	On-time
23 (young)	38,887 (average)	6,260	33,635	9,400	Low	Green	On-time
28 (young)	31,758 (average)	58,492	49,268	1,000	Low	Green	On-time
25 (young)	80,180 (high)	31,696	69,529	1,000	High	Green	Late
33 (middle)	40,921 (average)	91,111	90,076	2,900	Average	Yellow	Late
36 (middle)	63,124 (average)	164,631	144,697	300	Low	Green	On-time
39 (middle)	59,006 (average)	195,759	161,750	600	Low	Green	On-time
39 (middle)	125,713 (high)	382,180	315,396	5,200	Low	Yellow	On-time
55 (middle)	80,149 (high)	511,937	21,923	1,000	Low	Green	On-time
62 (old)	101,291 (high)	783,164	23,052	1,800	Low	Green	On-time
71 (old)	81,723 (high)	776,344	20,277	900	Low	Green	On-time
63 (old)	99,522 (high)	783,491	24,643	200	Low	Green	On-time

Table 4.5 Loan analysis test data

Age	Income	Assets	Debts	Want	Risk	Credit	Result
37 (middle)	37,214 (average)	123,420	106,241	4,100	Low	Green	On-time
45 (middle)	57,391 (average)	250,410	191,879	5,800	Low	Green	On-time
45 (middle)	36,692 (average)	175,037	137,800	3,400	Low	Green	On-time
25 (young)	67,808 (average)	25,174	61,271	3,100	High	Yellow	On-time
36 (middle)	102,143 (high)	246,148	231,334	600	Low	Green	On-time
29 (young)	34,579 (average)	49,387	59,412	4,600	High	Red	On-time
26 (young)	22,958 (low)	29,878	36,508	400	High	Yellow	Late
34 (middle)	42,526 (average)	109,934	92,494	3,700	Low	Green	On-time
28 (young)	80,019 (high)	78,632	100,957	12,800	High	Green	On-time
32 (middle)	57,407 (average)	117,062	101,967	100	Low	Green	On-time

Table 4.6 New appliance loan analysis

Age	Income	Assets	Debts	Want	Credit
25	28,650	9,824	2,000	10,000	Green
30	35,760	12,974	32,634	4,000	Yellow
32	41,862	625,321	428,643	3,000	Red
36	36,843	80,431	120,643	12,006	Green
37	62,743	421,753	321,845	5,000	Yellow
37	53,869	286,375	302,958	4,380	Green
37	70,120	484,264	303,958	6,000	Green
38	60,429	296,843	185,769	5,250	Green
39	65,826	321,959	392,817	12,070	Green
40	90,426	142,098	25,426	1,280	Yellow
40	70,256	528,493	283,745	3,280	Green
42	58,326	328,457	120,849	4,870	Green
42	61,242	525,673	184,762	3,300	Green
42	39,676	326,346	421,094	1,290	Red
43	102,496	823,532	175,932	3,370	Green
43	80,376	753,256	239,845	5,150	Yellow
44	74,623	584,234	398,456	1,525	Green
45	91,672	436,854	275,632	5,800	Green
52	120,721	921,482	128,573	2,500	Yellow
63	86,521	241,689	5,326	30,000	Green

	BusAd	Business Administration
	IS	Information Systems
Experience	integer	years of experience in this field
Outcome	ordinal	Unacceptable
		Minimal
		Adequate
		Excellent

Table 4.7 gives the 10 observations in the learning set.

Table 4.7 Job applicant training dataset

Record	Age	State	Degree	Major	Experience (in years)	Outcome
1	27	CA	BS	Engineering	2	Excellent
2	33	NV	MBA	Business Administration	5	Adequate
3	30	CA	MS	Computer Science	0	Adequate
4	22	CA	BS	Information Systems	0	Unacceptable
5	28	CA	BS	Information Systems	2	Minimal
6	26	CA	MS	Business Administration	0	Excellent
7	25	CA	BS	Engineering	3	Adequate
8	28	OR	MS	Computer Science	2	Adequate
9	25	CA	BS	Information Systems	2	Minimal
10	24	CA	BS	Information Systems	1	Adequate

Notice that some of these variables are quantitative and others are nominal. State, degree, and major are nominal. There is no information content intended by state or major. State is not expected to have a specific order prior to analysis, nor is major. (The analysis may conclude that there is a relationship between state, major, and outcome, however.) Degree is ordinal, in that MS and MBA are higher degrees than BS. However, as with state and major, the analysis may find a reverse relationship with the outcome.

Table 4.8 gives the test dataset for this case.

Table 4.9 provides a set of new job applicants to be classified by predicted job performance.

Insurance Fraud Data

The third dataset involves insurance claims. The full dataset includes 5,000 past claims with known outcomes. Variables include the claimant

Table 4.8 Job applicant test dataset

Record	Age	State	Degree	Major	Experience (in years)	Outcome
11	36	CA	MS	Information Systems	0	Minimal
12	28	OR	BS	Computer Science	5	Unacceptable
13	24	NV	BS	Information Systems	0	Excellent
14	33	CA	BS	Engineering	2	Adequate
15	26	CA	BS	Business Administration	3	Minimal

Table 4.9 New job applicant set

Age	State	Degree	Major	Experience (in years)
28	CA	MBA	Engr	0
26	NM	UG	Sci	3
33	TX	MS	Engr	6
21	CA	Cert	none	0
26	OR	Cert	none	5
25	CA	UG	BusAd	0
32	AR	UG	Engr	8
41	PA	MBA	BusAd	2
29	CA	UG	Sci	6
28	WA	UG	Csci	3

age, gender, amount of insurance claim, number of traffic tickets currently on record (less than 3 years old), number of prior accident claims of the type insured, and attorney (if any). Table 4.10 gives the training dataset.

The test set is given in Table 4.11.

A set of new claims is given in Table 4.12.

Table 4.10 Training dataset—Insurance claims

Claimant age	Gender	Claim amount	Tickets	Prior claims	Attorney	Outcome
52	Male	2,000	0	1	Jones	OK
38	Male	1,800	0	0	None	OK
21	Female	5,600	1	2	Smith	Fraudulent
36	Female	3,800	0	1	None	OK
19	Male	600	2	2	Adams	OK
41	Male	4,200	1	2	Smith	Fraudulent
38	Male	2,700	0	0	None	OK
33	Female	2,500	0	1	None	Fraudulent
18	Female	1,300	0	0	None	OK
26	Male	2,600	2	0	None	OK

Table 4.11 Test dataset—Insurance claims

Claimant age	Gender	Claim amount	Tickets	Prior claims	Attorney	Outcome
23	Male	2,800	1	0	None	OK
31	Female	1,400	0	0	None	OK
28	Male	4,200	2	3	Smith	Fraudulent
19	Male	2,800	0	1	None	OK
41	Male	1,600	0	0	Henry	OK

Table 4.12 New insurance claims

Claimant age	Gender	Claim amount	Tickets	Prior claims	Attorney
23	Male	1,800	1	1	None
32	Female	2,100	0	0	None
20	Female	1,600	0	0	None
18	Female	3,300	2	0	None
55	Male	4,000	0	0	Smith
41	Male	2,600	1	1	None
38	Female	3,100	0	0	None
21	Male	2,500	1	0	None
16	Female	4,500	1	2	Gold
24	Male	2,600	1	1	None

Expenditure Data

This dataset represents the consumer data for a community gathered by a hypothetical market research company in a moderate sized city. Ten thousand observations have been gathered over the following variables:

DEMOGRAPHIC
Age	integer, 16 and up
Gender	0-female, 1-male
Marital Status	0-single, 0.5-divorced, 1-married
Dependents	Number of dependents
Income	Annual income in dollars
Job yrs	Years in the current job (integer)
Town yrs	Years in this community
Yrs Ed	Years of education completed
Dri Lic	Drivers License (0-no, 1-yes)
Own Home	0-no, 1-yes
#Cred C	number of credit cards

CONSUMER
Churn	Number of credit card balances canceled last year
ProGroc	Proportion of income spent at grocery stores
ProRest	Proportion of income spent at restaurants
ProHous	Proportion of income spent on housing
ProUtil	Proportion of income spent on utilities
ProAuto	Proportion of income spent on automobiles (owned and operated)
ProCloth	Proportion of income spent on clothing
ProEnt	Proportion of income spent on entertainment

This dataset can be used for a number of studies to include questions, such as what types of customers are most likely to seek restaurants, what the market for home furnishings might be, what type of customers are most likely to be interested in clothing or in entertainment, and what is the relationship of spending to demographic variables.

Bankruptcy Data

This data concerns 100 U.S. firms that underwent bankruptcy.[1] All of the sample data are from the U.S. companies. About 400 bankrupt company names were obtained using google.com, and the next step is to find out the Ticker name of each company using the Compustat database, at the same time, we just kept the companies bankrupted during January 2006 and December 2009, since we hopefully want to get some different results because of this economic crisis. 99 companies left after this step. After getting the company the Ticker code list, we submitted the Ticker list to the Compustat database to get the financial data ratios during January 2005 to December 2009. Those financial data and ratios are the factors from which we can predict the company bankruptcy. The factors we collected are based on the literature, which contain total asset, book value per share, inventories, liabilities, receivables, cost of goods sold, total dividends, earnings before interest and taxes, gross profit (loss), net income (loss), operating income after depreciation, total revenue, sales, dividends per share, and total market value. We make a match for scale and size as 1:2 ratios. It means that we need to collect the same financial ratios for 200 nonfailed companies during the same periods. First, we used the LexisNexis database to find the company Securities and Exchange Commission filling after June 2010, which means that companies are still active today, and then, we selected 200 companies from the results and got the company CIK code list. The final step, we submitted the CIK code list to the Compustat database and got the financial data and ratios during January 2005 to December 2009, which is the same period with that of getting failed companies.

The dataset consists of 1,321 records with full data over 19 attributes, as shown in Table 4.13. The outcome attribute in bankruptcy has a value of 1 if the firm went bankrupt by 2011 (697 cases) and a value of 0 if it did not (624 cases).

This is real data concerning firm bankruptcy, which could be updated by going to the web sources.

Table 4.13 Attributes in bankruptcy data

No.	Short name	Long name
1	fyear	Data year—fiscal
2	cik	CIK number
3	at	Assets—total
4	bkvlps	Book value per share
5	invt	Inventories—total
6	Lt	Liabilities—total
7	rectr	Receivables—trade
8	cogs	Cost of goods sold
9	dvt	Dividends—total
10	ebit	Earnings before interest and taxes
11	gp	Gross profit (loss)
12	ni	Net income (loss)
13	oiadp	Operating income after depreciation
14	revt	Revenue—total
15	sale	Sales-turnover (net)
16	dvpsx_f	Dividends per share—ex-date—fiscal
17	mkvalt	Market value—total—fiscal
18	prch_f	Price high—annual—fiscal
19	bankruptcy	Bankruptcy (output variable)

Summary

There are a number of tools available for data mining, which can accomplish a number of functions. The tools come from areas of statistics, operations research, and artificial intelligence, providing analytical techniques that can be used to accomplish a variety of analytic functions, such as cluster identification, discriminant analysis, and development of association rules. Data mining software provides powerful means to apply these tools to large sets of data, giving the organizational management means to cope with an overwhelming glut of data and the ability to convert some of this glut into useful knowledge.

This chapter begins with an overview of tools and functions. It also previews four datasets that are used in subsequent chapters, plus a fifth dataset of real firm bankruptcies available for use. These datasets are small, but provide the readers with views of the type of data typically encountered in some data mining studies.

CHAPTER 5

Data Mining Software

There are many excellent commercial data mining software products, although these tend to be expensive. These include SAS Enterprise Miner and IBM's Intelligent Miner, as well as many more recent variants and new products appearing regularly. One source of information is www. kdnuggets.com under "software." Some of these are free. The most popular software by rdstats.com/articles/popularity by product are shown in Table 5.1.

Rattle is a graphical user interface (GUI) system for R (also open source), and is also highly recommended. WEKA is a great system, but we have found issues with reading test data, making it a bit troublesome. Down the list in 11th place is KNIME, a very easy-to-use open source GUI system that we will demonstrate. KNIME has the feature that it will read both R and WEKA models, along with the click-and-drag functionality to build workflows similar to SAS and SPSS products.

R

To install R, visit https://cran.rstudio.com/
Open a folder for R.
Select Download R for Windows.

Table 5.1 Data mining software by popularity (rdstats.com)

Rank		
1	R	Open source
2	SAS	Commercial
3	SPSS	Commercial
4	WEKA	Open source
5	Statistica	Commercial
5	Rapid Miner	Commercial

To install Rattle:

Open the R Desktop icon (32-bit or 64-bit) and enter the following command at the R prompt. R will ask for a CRAN mirror. Choose a nearby location.

```
> install.packages("rattle")
```

Enter the following two commands at the R prompt. This loads the Rattle package into the library and then starts up Rattle.

```
> library(rattle)
```

```
> rattle()
```

If the RGtk2 package is yet to be installed, there will be an error popup indicating that libatk-1.0-0.dll is missing from your computer. Click on the OK button and then, you will be asked if you would like to install GTK+. Click on OK to do so. This then downloads and installs the appropriate GTK+ libraries for your computer. After this has finished, do exit from R and restart it so that it can find the newly installed libraries.

When running Rattle, a number of other packages will be downloaded and installed as needed, with Rattle asking for the user's permission before doing so. They only need to be downloaded once.

The installation has been tested to work on Microsoft Windows, 32-bit and 64-bit, XP, Vista, and 7 with R 3.1.1, Rattle 3.1.0, and RGtk2 2.20.31. If you are missing something, you will get a message from R asking you to install a package. I read nominal data (string), and was prompted that I needed "stringr." On the R console (see Figure 5.1), click on the "Packages" tab on the top line.

Give the command "Install packages," which will direct you to HTTPS CRAN mirror. Select one of the sites (like "USA(TX) [https]") and find "stringr" and click on it. Then, upload that package. You may have to restart R.

To run a model, on the *Filename* line, click on the icon and browse for the file "LoanRaw.csv." Click on the *Execute* icon on the upper left of the Rattle window. This yields Figure 5.2.

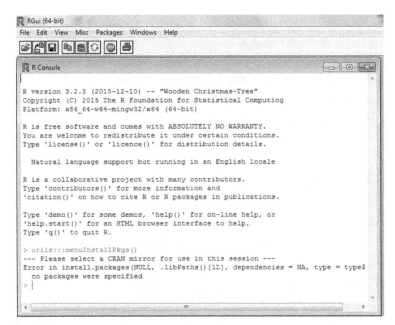

Figure 5.1 R console

Figure 5.2 LoanRaw.csv data read

We can *Explore*—the default is *Summary*. *Execute* yields Figure 5.3. Figure 5.3 shows the output.

Here variable "Risk" is a function "Assets," "Debt," and "Want." Rattle treated "Debt" as an identifier variable and deleted it from the analysis. This can be adjusted by the user so desires.

Select the *Model* tab, yielding Figure 5.4.

This yields options to set parameters for a decision tree, which we will examine later in the book. For now, we can use the default settings shown, *Execute*, and obtain Figure 5.5.

Rattle can also provide a descriptive decision tree by selecting the *Rules* button, yielding Figure 5.6.

Selecting the *Draw* button yields Figure 5.7, a graphic decision tree.

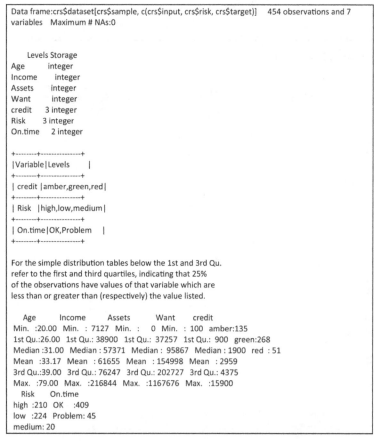

```
Data frame:crs$dataset[crs$sample, c(crs$input, crs$risk, crs$target)]   454 observations and 7
variables   Maximum # NAs:0


      Levels Storage
Age       integer
Income     integer
Assets     integer
Want       integer
credit    3 integer
Risk      3 integer
On.time    2 integer


+--------+---------------+
|Variable|Levels    |
+--------+---------------+
| credit |amber,green,red|
+--------+---------------+
| Risk  |high,low,medium|
+--------+---------------+
| On.time|OK,Problem   |
+--------+---------------+

For the simple distribution tables below the 1st and 3rd Qu.
refer to the first and third quartiles, indicating that 25%
of the observations have values of that variable which are
less than or greater than (respectively) the value listed.

    Age       Income     Assets     Want      credit
Min.  :20.00  Min. : 7127  Min. :    0  Min. : 100  amber:135
1st Qu.:26.00  1st Qu.: 38900  1st Qu.: 37257  1st Qu.: 900  green:268
Median :31.00  Median : 57371  Median : 95867  Median : 1900  red : 51
Mean  :33.17  Mean  : 61655  Mean  : 154998  Mean  : 2959
3rd Qu.:39.00  3rd Qu.: 76247  3rd Qu.: 202727  3rd Qu.: 4375
Max.  :79.00  Max.  :216844  Max. :1167676  Max. :15900
    Risk     On.time
high :210  OK   :409
low  :224  Problem: 45
medium: 20
```

Figure 5.3 Summary of LoanRaw.csv

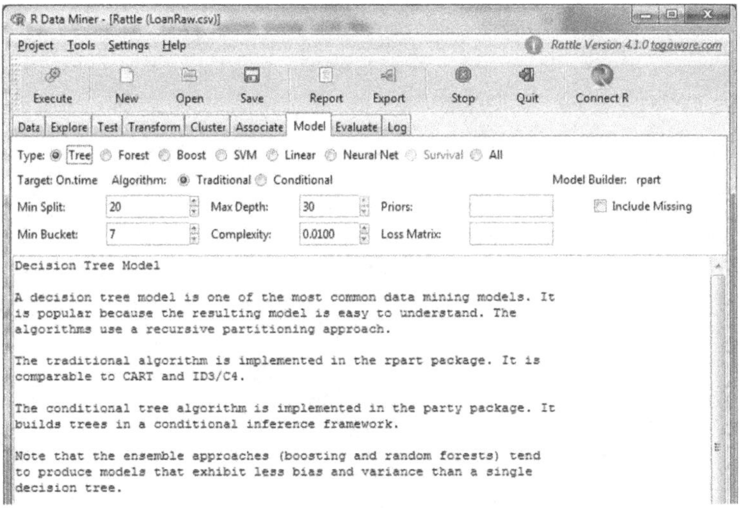

Figure 5.4 Model tab with Tree selected

Figure 5.5 Decision tree model for LoanRaw.csv data

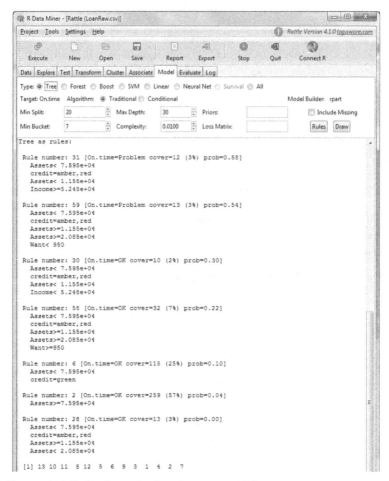

Figure 5.6 Rules from the decision tree model

This just provides an initial glimpse of what R (through Rattle) can provide. We will demonstrate the analysis in greater depth in subsequent chapters.

KNIME

To install KNIME, you have to log into tech.knime.org/user, getting a username and password. You then can proceed to installation. Table 5.2 describes the KNIME versions and on which platform they are available.

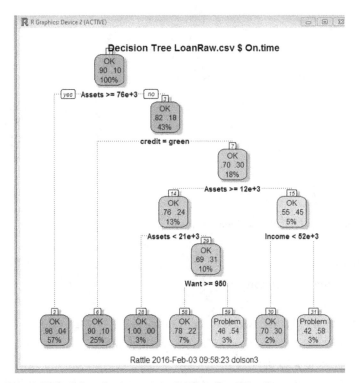

Figure 5.7 *Graphic decision tree display from Rattle*

Table 5.2 *KNIME versions (from their website)*

	Linux	Windows	Mac OS X
KNIME (32-bit)	Yes	Yes	No
KNIME (64-bit)	Yes	Yes	Yes
KNIME Developer Version (32-bit)	Yes	Yes	No
KNIME Developer Version (64-bit)	Yes	Yes	Yes

Installation is accomplished by:

Download one of the aforementioned versions, unzip it to any directory. For Windows, click on the *knime.exe* file, and for Linux, click on *knime* in order to start KNIME. When KNIME is started for the first time, a welcome screen (Figure 5.8) appears.

Figure 5.8 KNIME welcome screen

From here, you can

1. Open KNIME workbench: Opens the KNIME workbench to immediately start exploring KNIME, build own workflows, and explore your data.
2. Get additional nodes: In addition to the ready-to-start basic KNIME installation, there are additional plug-ins for KNIME, for example, an R and Weka integration, or the integration of the Chemistry Development Kit with the additional nodes for the processing of chemical structures, compounds, and so on. You can download these features later from within KNIME (File, Update KNIME) as well.

The KNIME workbench is organized as in Figure 5.9.

A workflow is built by dragging the nodes from the Node Repository to the Workflow Editor and connecting them. Nodes are the basic processing units of a workflow. Each node has a number of input and output ports. Data (or a model) is transferred via a connection from an out-port to the in-port of another node.

Node Status

When a node is dragged to the workflow editor, the status light lights up red, which means that the node has to be configured in order to be able to

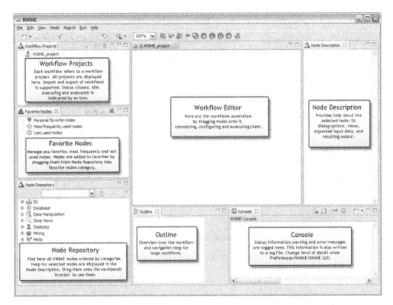

Figure 5.9 KNIME workflow

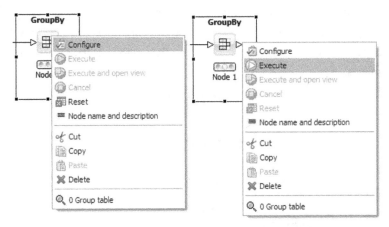

Figure 5.10 KNIME configuration

be executed. A node is configured by right-clicking it, choosing *Configure*, and adjusting the necessary settings in the node's dialog, as displayed in Figure 5.10.

When the dialog is closed by clicking on the *OK* button, the node is configured and the status light changes to yellow: the node is ready to be executed. Right-clicking the node again shows an enabled *Execute* option;

clicking on it will execute the node and the result of this node will be available at the out-port. After a successful execution, the status light of the node is green. The result(s) can be inspected by exploring the out-port view(s): the last entries in the context menu open them.

Ports

The ports on the left are input ports, where the data from the out-port of the predecessor node is provided. The ports on the right are out-ports. The result of the node's operation on the data is provided at the out-port to successor nodes. A tooltip provides information about the output of the node, further information can be found in the node description. Nodes are typed such that only ports of the same type can be connected.

Data Port

Figure 5.11 shows the most common type, the data port (a white triangle), which transfers flat data tables from node to node.

Figure 5.12 shows a database port: Nodes executing commands inside a database are recognized by these database ports displayed as brown squares.

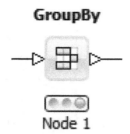

Figure 5.11 KNIME data port

Figure 5.12 KNIME database port

Figure 5.13 KNIME PMML port

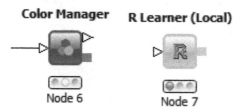

Figure 5.14 Other KNIME ports

Data mining nodes learn a model, which is passed to the referring predictor node via a blue squared PMML port (Figure 5.13).

Whenever a node provides data that does not fit a flat data table structure, a general purpose port for structured data is used (dark cyan square). All ports not listed earlier are known as "unknown" types (gray square), as in Figure 5.14.

Opening a New Workflow

We can open a new workflow for LoanRaw.csv. We first input the data, by clicking and dragging a *File Reader* node. We enter the location of the file by clicking on *Browse ...* and locating the file. Figure 5.15 exhibits this operation.

Click on the *File Reader* node and select *Apply* followed by *OK*. Then, click on *File Reader* (which now should have a yellow status light) and click on *Execute*. If all is well, the status light will change to green. This enables linkage to other nodes. Click-and-drag the *Decision Tree Learner* node and link it to the File Reader icon. Click on this Decision Tree

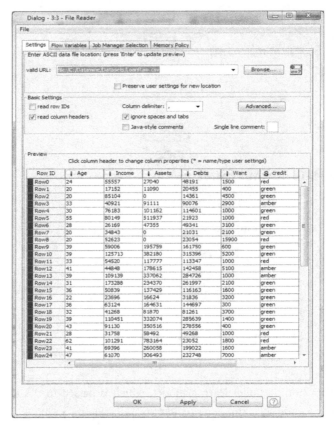

Figure 5.15 Opening LoanRaw.csv

Learner node and select *Apply* followed by *OK*. Then, click on the icon again and select *Execute*. The status light should change to green.

In Chapter 3, we discussed a data mining process, where it is a good practice to build the model on one set of data, and then test it on another subset of data. The purpose of building data mining models is to have them available to predict new cases. Figure 5.16 shows the KNIME workflow process.

In Figure 5.16, we demonstrate a complete process where a training set is read into the first File Reader and the Decision Tree Learner is used to build a model. This feeds into the Decision Tree Predictor node, which is linked to another File Reader node with test data. The Decision Tree Predictor node feeds into a Scorer node, which provides

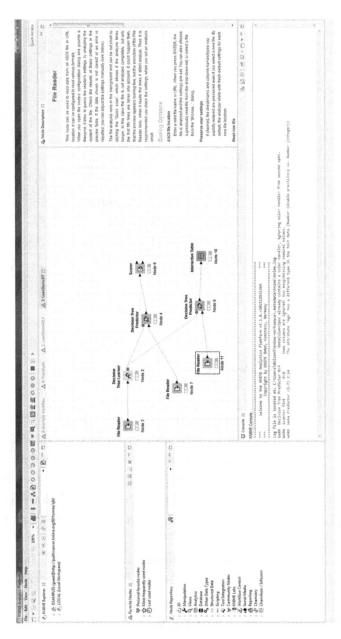

Figure 5.16 KNIME LoanRaw.csv decision tree process

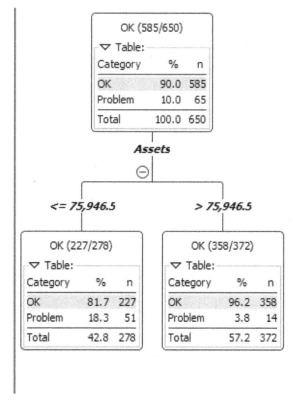

Figure 5.17 KNIME decision tree

a confusion matrix, displaying model fit on the test data. To apply this model to new data, a third File Reader node is where new cases are linked, feeding into another Decision Tree Predictor node (linked to the Decision Tree Learner model), providing output to an Interactive Table providing model predictions for the new cases. In the Decision Tree Learner node, we apply *Pruning* of *MDL*. Right-clicking on the node, we obtain the following decision tree (Figure 5.17).

We will demonstrate KNIME throughout the book. We also add WEKA installation, as it has great tools for data mining algorithms.

WEKA

WEKA (you can download off the Web) www.cs.waikato.ac.nz/ml/weka/. The download comes with documentation.

On WEKA:

Hit the Open file ... button on the upper left.

Link to LoanRaw.csv (or any .csv or .arff file you want to analyze).

Install—hopefully, you get Figure 5.18.

Select *Explorer*, yielding Figure 5.19.

Select *Open file ...* and pick file from your hard drive. In Figure 5.20, we picked *LoanRaw.csv*.

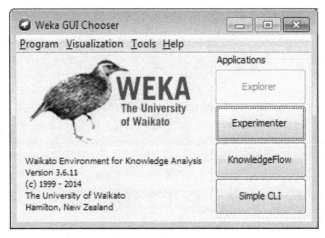

Figure 5.18 WEKA opening screen

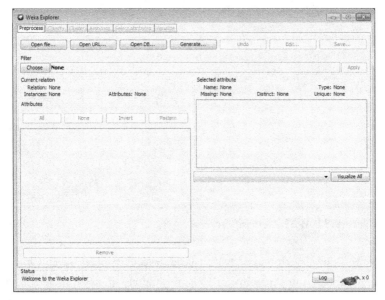

Figure 5.19 WEKA explorer screen

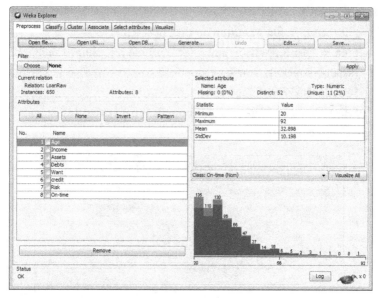

Figure 5.20 WEKA screen for LoanRaw.csv

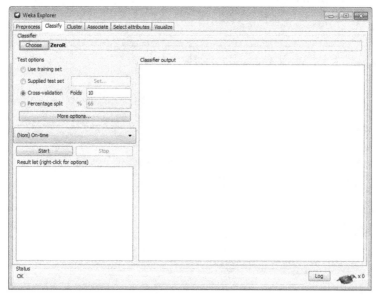

Figure 5.21 WEKA classify screen

You can play around with Visualized, Select attributes, (even Cluster or Associate), but the point for us is to build classification models with *Classify*, as in Figure 5.21.

Select *Choose* to get Figure 5.22.

Select *Trees* to get Figure 5.23.

Figure 5.22 WEKA explorer classification algorithm menu

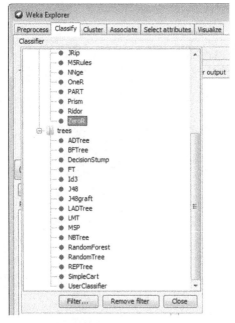

Figure 5.23 WEKA tree algorithm menu

There are 16 different decision tree models. The interesting ones for us are J48 and SimpleCart.

If you select J48, and then click on the *Choose* line (with J48 C 0.25 M 2), you get a control window, as in Figure 5.24.

You can change the confidence factor of the algorithm (requiring a minimum level of confidence before retaining a rule) and the minimum number of cases for a rule (called support). This provides a means to try to adjust the number of decision tree rules.

To run a J48 model (with defaults of C=0.25 and M=2), select *OK* in Figure 5.25.

Select *Start*.

This yields Figure 5.26.

The result is a tree with no rules—it cheats and says all loan applications are OK (it is wrong 65 times out of 650, giving a correct classification rate of 0.90). I call this a degenerate model—it just says everything is OK.

To get a more interesting model, play with C and M.

For C=0.5 and M=6, I get Figure 5.27.

The actual tree is more compactly shown in Figure 5.28.

Figure 5.24 WEKA J48 parameter settings

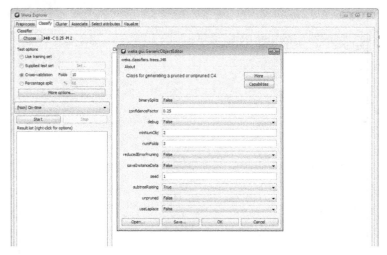

Figure 5.25 Running J48 decision tree

This tree has six leaves (ways this rule set has to reach a conclusion)—note that you can shorten that—here, I did it in 2. It has a tree size of 9 (rows to express the rule set—although here I count 8)—tree size doesn't mean much.

Hit the *Choose* button

Under Functions, you can select

    Logistic for logistic regression

    Multilayer perceptron or RBF Network for neural network

Trees

    J48 for a good tree

    Decision Stump for a simple

    SimpleCart

For J48, you can control the number of rules by manipulating parameter M (which is the minimum number of cases required in order to build a rule).

If Output Variable Is Continuous

Functions

    Linear regression

Trees

    M5P gives a tree of multiple linear regressions

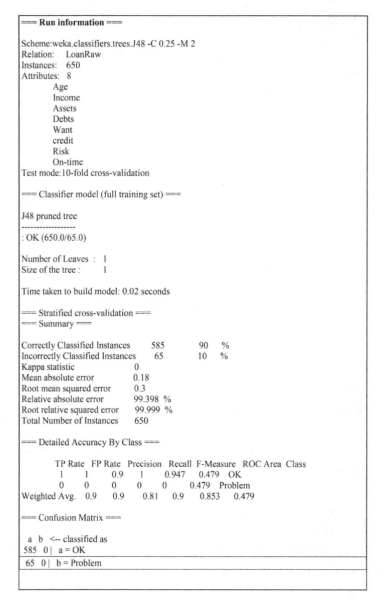

=== Run information ===

Scheme:weka.classifiers.trees.J48 -C 0.25 -M 2
Relation: LoanRaw
Instances: 650
Attributes: 8
          Age
          Income
          Assets
          Debts
          Want
          credit
          Risk
          On-time
Test mode:10-fold cross-validation

=== Classifier model (full training set) ===

J48 pruned tree

: OK (650.0/65.0)

Number of Leaves :   1
Size of the tree :   1

Time taken to build model: 0.02 seconds

=== Stratified cross-validation ===
=== Summary ===

Correctly Classified Instances   585   90   %
Incorrectly Classified Instances   65   10   %
Kappa statistic   0
Mean absolute error   0.18
Root mean squared error   0.3
Relative absolute error   99.398 %
Root relative squared error   99.999 %
Total Number of Instances   650

=== Detailed Accuracy By Class ===

          TP Rate FP Rate Precision Recall F-Measure ROC Area Class
            1   1   0.9   1   0.947   0.479   OK
            0   0   0   0   0   0.479   Problem
Weighted Avg. 0.9   0.9   0.81   0.9   0.853   0.479

=== Confusion Matrix ===

  a   b   <-- classified as
585   0 | a = OK
 65   0 | b = Problem

Figure 5.26 J48 output for LoanRaw.csv

Select the button for *Use training data* or *Cross-validation* with 10 folds, or *Percentage split.*

WEKA will give you a decision tree. Under *Trees,* you can select a variety of decision tree models, to include J48 (requires categorical output).

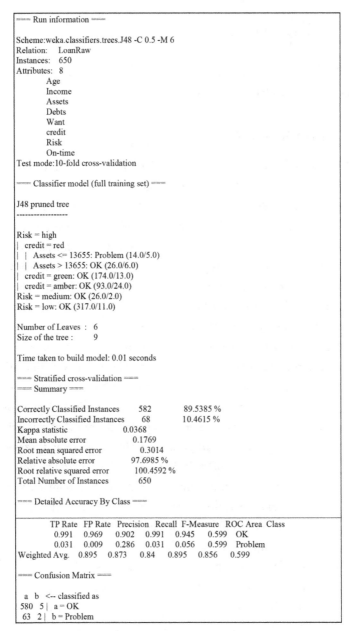

```
=== Run information ===

Scheme:weka.classifiers.trees.J48 -C 0.5 -M 6
Relation:    LoanRaw
Instances:   650
Attributes:  8
        Age
        Income
        Assets
        Debts
        Want
        credit
        Risk
        On-time
Test mode:10-fold cross-validation

=== Classifier model (full training set) ===

J48 pruned tree
------------------

Risk = high
|  credit = red
|  |  Assets <= 13655: Problem (14.0/5.0)
|  |  Assets > 13655: OK (26.0/6.0)
|  credit = green: OK (174.0/13.0)
|  credit = amber: OK (93.0/24.0)
Risk = medium: OK (26.0/2.0)
Risk = low: OK (317.0/11.0)

Number of Leaves :   6
Size of the tree :      9

Time taken to build model: 0.01 seconds

=== Stratified cross-validation ===
=== Summary ===

Correctly Classified Instances      582           89.5385 %
Incorrectly Classified Instances     68           10.4615 %
Kappa statistic                      0.0368
Mean absolute error                  0.1769
Root mean squared error              0.3014
Relative absolute error             97.6985 %
Root relative squared error        100.4592 %
Total Number of Instances           650

=== Detailed Accuracy By Class ===

          TP Rate  FP Rate  Precision  Recall  F-Measure  ROC Area  Class
          0.991    0.969    0.902      0.991   0.945      0.599     OK
          0.031    0.009    0.286      0.031   0.056      0.599     Problem
Weighted Avg.  0.895  0.873  0.84     0.895   0.856      0.599

=== Confusion Matrix ===

  a   b   <-- classified as
580   5 |  a = OK
 63   2 |  b = Problem
```

Figure 5.27 Modified J48 decision tree

For data files containing only continuous data, you can use Decision Stump or M5P. The answer you get in that case will be an estimate of the proportion of the outcome variable.

```
IF RISK=HIGH
        AND IF CREDIT=Red
                AND IF Assets ≤ 13655 THEN Problem (there was a problem in 14 of 19
such cases)
ELSE OK
```

Figure 5.28 Compact tree for Figure 5.27

To Predict Within WEKA

This is the hardest thing about WEKA. There is a way to apply the neural net model to test cases, but it is cumbersome. Generally, I've found that using a supplied test set works pretty well for generating the predictions that use only numeric data (e.g., expenditure files). You have to make sure the header rows match exactly and add any "actual" value for the independent variable column (our assignments have not provided an actual value for test cases). You have to make sure the data structures match exactly, so in the case of the expenditure files, there are some text fields that have to be converted into numeric values.

WEKA doesn't handle text data as cleanly, but it can be done. I appended the test cases to the training .csv file and saved with a different name. All text values have to match exactly to the training set (–e.g., Undergrad = UG, None = none, etc.). It is case-sensitive, which adds to the difficulty. Load the training set (this part is the same for numeric or text). From *Test* options, use *Supplied test set* (click on *Set* and browse to find the file). Then, go to *More options* and click on *Output predictions*. Run the model and the predictions appear above the Summary. WEKA will give predictions (what the model projects) and actuals (what was in the dataset) for all observations. The added data will be at the end, so you only have to scroll up above the confusion matrix.

When that fails, one thing that seems to work is:

To the original dataset, add the new cases at the bottom (making sure that the spelling is the same).

Have the original data set loaded (Figure 5.29).

When you select the model, instead of 10-fold testing, click on *Supply test set* and link the file with the 10 cases at the bottom.

Under *More options*, select *Output Predictions*.

When you then run the model, the predictions (for all 510) will be listed above the confusion matrix (Figure 5.30). The "actual" will be phony—but the "predicted" will be there.

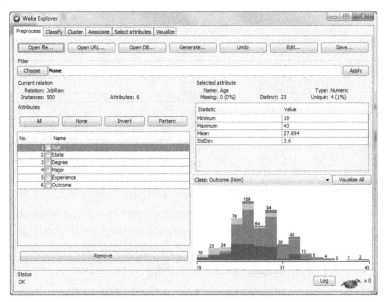

Figure 5.29 Original data load—LoanRaw.csv

```
OUTPUT: instance, actual, prediction, error stuff  (the "excellen" actuals were dummies)
  501 4:excellen 2:adequate    +  0.04 *0.886 0    0.074
  502 4:excellen 4:excellen       0.004 0.262 0   *0.734
  503 4:excellen 2:adequate    +  0.004 *0.92 0    0.076
  504 4:excellen 2:adequate    +  0.025 *0.588 0   0.387
  505 4:excellen 3:unaccept    +  0.41 0.013 *0.577 0
  506 4:excellen 1:minimal     +  *0.594 0.383 0.024 0
  507 4:excellen 2:adequate    +  0.313 *0.603 0.084 0
  508 4:excellen 4:excellen       0.002 0.228 0    *0.77
  509 4:excellen 2:adequate    +  0.164 *0.827 0.009 0
  510 4:excellen 3:unaccept    +  0   0   *1   0

=== Evaluation on test set ===
=== Summary ===

Correctly Classified Instances        336            65.8824 %
Incorrectly Classified Instances      174            34.1176 %
Kappa statistic                       0.4285
Mean absolute error                   0.2063
Root mean squared error               0.3249
Relative absolute error               66.6581 %
Root relative squared error           82.2284 %
Total Number of Instances             510

=== Detailed Accuracy By Class ===

              TP Rate  FP Rate  Precision  Recall  F-Measure  ROC Area  Class
              0.581    0.211    0.545      0.581   0.563      0.823     minimal
              0.817    0.304    0.741      0.817   0.778      0.858     adequate
              0.39     0.049    0.511      0.39    0.442      0.91      unacceptable
              0.242    0.004    0.8        0.242   0.372      0.84      excellent
Weighted Avg. 0.659    0.227    0.659      0.659   0.647      0.852
```

Figure 5.30 Prediction output (Continued)

```
=== Confusion Matrix ===

 a   b   c  d  <-- classified as
90  48  17  0 |  a = minimal
43 215   3  2 |  b = adequate
31   5  23  0 |  c = unacceptable
 1  22   2  8 |  d = excellent
```

Figure 5.30 Prediction output

Summary

There are many excellent data mining software products, commercial (which are often expensive, but quite easy to use) as well as open source. WEKA was one of the earlier open source products. R has grown to be viable for major data mining, and the Rattle GUI makes it easy to implement. KNIME is newer and has some of the click-and-drag features that made commercial software so easy to use.

CHAPTER 6

Regression Algorithms in Data Mining

Regression is a basic statistical tool. In data mining, it is one of the basic tools for analysis used in the classification applications through logistic regression and discriminant analysis, as well as the prediction of continuous data through ordinary least squares (OLS) and other forms. As such, regression is often taught in one (or more) three-hour courses. We cannot hope to cover all of the basics of regression. However, we, here, present ways in which regression is used within the context of data mining.

Regression is used on a variety of data types. If data is time series, the output from regression models is often used for forecasting. Regression can be used to build predictive models for other types of data. Regression can be applied in a number of different forms. The class of regression models is a major class of tools available to support the Modeling phase of the data mining process.

Probably, the most widely used data mining algorithms are data fitting, in the sense of regression. Regression is a fundamental tool for statistical analysis to characterize relationships between a dependent variable and one or more independent variables. Regression models can be used for many purposes, to include explanation and prediction. *Linear* and *logistic* regression models are both primary tools in most general-purpose data mining software. Nonlinear data can sometimes be transformed into useful linear data and analyzed with linear regression. Some special forms of nonlinear regression also exist. *Neural network* models are also widely used for the same classes of models. Both regression and neural network models require data be expressed numerically (or at least as 0 to 1 dummy variables). The primary operational difference between regression and neural networks is that regression provides a formula that has a strong body of theory behind it for application and interpretation.

Neural networks generally do not provide models for interpretation and are usually applied internally within the software that built the model. In this sense, neural networks appear to users as "black boxes" that classify or predict without explanation. There are, of course, the models behind these classifications and predictions, but they tend to be so complex that they are neither printed out nor analyzed.

Regression Models

OLS regression is a model of the form:

$$Y = \beta_0 + \beta_1 X_1 + \beta_2 X_2 + \ldots + \beta_n X_n + \varepsilon$$

where, Y is the dependent variable (the one being forecast)

X_n are the n independent (explanatory) variables

β_0 is the intercept term

β_n are the n coefficients for the independent variables

ε is the error term

OLS regression is a straight line (with intercept and slope coefficients β_n), which minimizes the sum of squared error terms ε_i over all i observations. The idea is that you look at past data to determine the β coefficients that worked best. The model gives you the most likely future value of the dependent variable, given knowledge of the X_n for future observations. This approach assumes a linear relationship, and error terms that are normally distributed around zero without patterns. While these assumptions are often unrealistic, regression is highly attractive because of the existence of the widely available computer packages as well as highly developed statistical theory. The statistical packages provide the probability that estimated parameters differ from zero.

Classical Tests of the Regression Model

The universal test for classification in data mining is the coincidence matrix that focuses on the ability of the model to categorize the data. For continuous regression, this requires identification of cutoffs between the classes. Data mining software doesn't do that, but we will demonstrate how it can be done. There are many other aspects to accuracy, just as there are many applications of different models, especially regression. The classical tests of regression models are based on the assumption that errors are normally distributed around the mean, with no patterns. The basis of regression accuracy is the residuals, or difference between the predicted and observed values. Residuals are then extended to a general measure of regression fit, R-squared.

Linear Discriminant Analysis

Discriminant analysis groups objects defined by a set of variables into a predetermined set of outcome classes. One example of this type of analysis is the classification of employees by their rated performance within an organization. The bank loan example could be divided into past cases sorted by the two distinct categories of repayment or default. The technical analysis is, thus, determining the combination of variables that best predict membership in one of the given output categories.

A number of methods can be used for discriminant analysis. Regression can be used for discriminant analysis. For the two group case, this would require a cutoff between the groups, and if a new set of data yielded a functional value below the cutoff, the prediction would be that group, or conversely, if the value was above the cutoff, the prediction would be the other group. However, other techniques can be used for discriminant analysis.[1] A discriminant function can be used in binary data to separate observations into two groups, with a cutoff limit used to divide the observations.

Logistic Regression

Some data of interest in a regression study may be ordinal or nominal. For instance, in our example job application model, sex and college degree are nominal. In the loan application data, the outcome is nominal, while credit rating is ordinal. Since regression analysis requires numerical data, we included them by *coding* the variables. Here, each of these variables is dichotomous; therefore, we can code them as either 0 or 1 (as we did in the regression model for loan applicants). For example, a male is assigned a code of 0, while a female is assigned a code of 1. The employees with a college degree can be assigned a code of 1, and those without a degree a code of 0.

The purpose of logistic regression is to classify cases into the most likely category. Logistic regression provides a set of β parameters for the intercept (or intercepts in the case of ordinal data with more than two categories) and independent variables, which can be applied to a logistic function to estimate the probability of belonging to a specified output class. The formula for probability of acceptance of a case i to a stated class j is:

$$P_j = \frac{1}{1 + e^{\left(-\beta_0 - \sum \beta_i x_i\right)}}$$

where, β coefficients are obtained from logistic regression.

The regression model provides a continuous formula. A cutoff needs to be determined to divide the value obtained from this formula, given independent variable values, which will divide the data into output categories in proportion to the population of cases.

Chapter 4 included a set of data for insurance claims, some of which were fraudulent. The independent variables included the claimant age, gender, claim amount, number of traffic tickets on record, number of prior claims, and attorney. Here, we simplify the attorney data to focus on attorney Smith, making it a 0 to1 variable. Table 6.1 provides 10 observations, reflecting that data given in Table 4.10.

A logistic regression model was developed for this data using SAS, yielding the model given in Table 6.2. This report gives the model in terms of coefficients for the intercept and each variable (the *Estimate* column) with the standard error of each estimate. Since the logistic regression is based on discrete values for some variables, a chi-squared test is conventional for evaluation of each model coefficient (given in the *Chi-Square* column). The evaluation of these coefficients is the easiest to understand by viewing the last column, giving the probability of a random measure being greater than the chi-squared value. If this probability is high, the implication is that the coefficient is not very significant. If this probability is very low (or near zero), the implication is that the coefficient is significant.

Table 6.1 Insurance claim training data

Age	Gender	Claim	Tickets	Prior	Attorney	Outcome
52	0	2,000	0	1	0	OK
38	0	1,800	0	0	0	OK
21	1	5,600	1	2	1	Fraud
36	1	3,800	0	1	0	OK
19	0	600	2	2	0	OK
41	0	4,200	1	2	1	Fraud
38	0	2,700	0	0	0	OK
33	1	2,500	0	1	0	Fraud
18	1	1,300	0	0	0	OK
26	0	2,600	2	0	0	OK

Table 6.2 Logistic regression model for insurance claim data

Parameter	Estimate	Std. error	Chi-square	Pr>ChiSq
Intercept	81.624	309.3	0.0697	0.7918
Age	−2.778	10.4	0.0713	0.7894
Gender	−75.893	246.7	0.0946	0.7584
Claim	0.017	0.055	0.0959	0.7569
Tickets	−36.648	164.5	0.0496	0.8237
Prior	6.914	84.8	0.0067	0.9350
Smith?	−29.361	103.3	0.0809	0.7761

The *Estimate* column gives the model β coefficients. This model can be applied to the test data set given in Table 4.11 by using the probability formula given earlier. The calculations are shown in Table 6.3.

The coincidence matrix for this set of data is given in Table 6.4.

In this case, the model identified the one actually fraudulent case, at the expense of overpredicting the fraud.

Software Demonstrations

For OLS regression, both SAS and Excel were demonstrated earlier. Both obviously provide identical models. The only limitation we perceive to using Excel is that Excel regression is limited to 16 independent variables.

Table 6.3 *Logistic regression model applied to insurance fraud test cases*

Age	Gender	Claim	Tickets	Prior	Attorney	Model	Prob	Predict	Actual
23	0	2,800	1	0	0	28.958	1.0	OK	OK
31	1	1,400	0	0	0	−56.453	0.0	Fraud	OK
28	0	4,200	2	3	1	−6.261	0.002	Fraud	Fraud
19	0	2,800	0	1	0	83.632	1.0	OK	OK
41	0	1,600	0	0	0	−4.922	0.007	Fraud	OK

Table 6.4 *Coincidence matrix for insurance fraud data using logistic regression*

Actual	Fraud	OK	Total
Fraud	1	0	1
OK	2	2	4
Totals	3	2	0.60

The basic SAS has the ability to do OLS regression (so does Excel) and logistic regression.

The first 4,000 observations of the insurance fraud dataset were used for training. Standardized scores (between 0 and 1) were used, although continuous data, or even categorical data, could have been used. Standardizing the data transforms it so that scale doesn't matter. There are reasons to do that, if different variables have radically different scales. Regression results should be identical between standardized and original data (standardized data is continuous, just like the original—it is just transformed). As a check, you could run against the original data and see if you get the same R-squared and t statistics. The coefficients will be different. Categorical data is transformed into a form where details are lost. You will get different results between regressions over original continuous data and categorical data.

Regression Discriminant Model: For the regression model over standardized data, the result was as shown in Table 6.5:

Table 6.5 OLS regression output—Insurance fraud data

Summary output						
Regression statistics						
Multiple R	0.203298					
R square	0.04133					
Adjusted R square	0.03989					
Standard error	0.119118					
Observations	4,000					
ANOVA						
	df	*SS*	*MS*	*F*	*Significance F*	
Regression	6	2.442607	0.407101	28.69096	8.81E-34	
Residual	3,993	56.65739	0.014189			
Total	3,999	59.1				

(Continued)

Table 6.5 OLS regression output—Insurance fraud data (Continued)

	Coeffi-cients	Standard error	t Stat	P-value	Lower 95%	Upper 95%
Intercept	0.0081	0.012594	0.643158	0.520158	−0.01659	0.032792
Age	0.001804	0.005147	0.350421	0.726041	−0.00829	0.011894
Gender	−0.00207	0.003772	−0.54928	0.582843	−0.00947	0.005323
Claim	0.007607	0.0191	0.398289	0.690438	−0.02984	0.045054
Tickets	−0.0076	0.004451	−1.70738	0.08783	−0.01633	0.001127
Prior	0.000148	0.004174	0.035408	0.971756	−0.00804	0.008332
Attorney	0.201174	0.018329	10.97554	1.24E-27	0.165238	0.237109

Table 6.6 Coincidence matrix—OLS regression of insurance fraud test data

Actual	Model fraud	Model OK	Total
Fraud	5	17	22
OK	17	961	978
Totals	22	978	1,000

Of course, the same model was obtained with SAS. Only the presence of an attorney (highly significant) and number of tickets on record (marginally significant) had any significance. The β coefficients give the discriminant function. A cutoff value for this function is needed. We applied the model to the training set and sorted the results. There were 60 fraudulent cases in the training set of 4,000 observations. Therefore, a logical cutoff would be the 60th largest functional value in this training set. The 60th largest model value was 0.196197. The cutoff for prediction of 0.19615 was used. This yielded the coincidence matrix shown in Table 6.6.

This model had a correct classification rate of 0.966, which is very good. The model applied to the test data predicted 22 fraudulent cases, and 978 not fraudulent. Of the 22 test cases that the model predicted to be fraudulent, 5 actually were. Therefore, the model would have triggered investigation of 17 cases in the test set, which were not actually fraudulent. Of the 978 test cases that the model predicted to be OK, 17 were actually fraudulent and would not have been investigated. If the cost of an investigation were $500, and the cost of loss were $2,500, this would have an expected cost of $500 × 17 + $2,500 × 17, or $51,000.

Centroid Discriminant Model: We can compare this model with a centroid discriminant model. The training set is used to identify the mean variable values for the two outcomes (Fraud and OK) shown in Table 6.7.

The squared distance to each of these clusters was applied on the 1,000 test observations, yielding the coincidence matrix shown in Table 6.8.

Here, the correct classification rate was 0.852, quite a bit lower than with the regression model. The model had many errors, where applicants who turned out to be OK were denied loans. There were two fewer cases, where applicants who turned out bad were approved for loans. The cost of error here is $500 × 133 + $2,500 × 15, or $104,000.

Logistic Regression Model: A logistic regression model was run on SAS. The variables Gender and Attorney were 0 to1 variables, and thus categorical. The model, based on the maximum likelihood estimates, is given in Table 6.9.

The outputs obtained were all between 0 and 1, but the maximum was 0.060848. The division between the 60th and 61st largest training values was 0.028. Using this cutoff, the coincidence matrix shown in Table 6.10 was obtained.

The correct classification rate is up very slightly, to 0.967. The cost of error here is $500 × 16 + $2,500 × 17, or $50,500.

Table 6.7 Centroid discriminant function means

Cluster	Age	Gender	Claim	Tickets	Prior	Attorney
OK	0.671	0.497	0.606	0.068	0.090	0.012
Fraud	0.654	0.467	0.540	0.025	0.275	0.217

Table 6.8 Coincidence matrix—centroid discriminant model of insurance fraud test data

Actual	Model fraud	Model OK	Total
Fraud	7	15	22
OK	133	845	978
Totals	140	860	1,000

Table 6.9 Logistic regression model—Insurance fraud data

Parameter	DF	Estimate	Std. error	Chi-square	Pr>ChiSq
Intercept	1	−2.9821	0.7155	17.3702	<0.0001
Age	1	0.1081	0.3597	0.0903	0.7637
Claim	1	0.3219	1.2468	0.0667	0.7962
Tickets	1	−0.8535	0.5291	2.6028	0.1067
Prior	1	0.0033	0.3290	0.0001	0.9920
Gender 0	1	0.0764	0.1338	0.3260	0.5680
Attorney 0	1	−1.6429	0.4107	15.9989	<0.0001

Table 6.10 Coincidence matrix—Logistic regression of insurance fraud data

Actual	Model fraud	Model OK	Total
Fraud	5	17	22
OK	16	962	978
Totals	21	979	1,000

The Job Application dataset involves 500 cases. Since there are four distinct outcomes, discriminant analysis is appropriate. (Cluster analysis might have been appropriate to identify these four outcomes in the first place.) We will use 250 cases for training, and test on the remaining 250. Excel turns out to be very easy to use for distance calculation. The first step is to convert data into a 0–1 scale (see Table 6.11).

In Excel, we place the outcome variable to the left of the four columns with the converted data, so that we can sort the 250 training observations on outcome. This simplifies the calculation of averages for each of the four variables by each of the four outcomes. Table 6.12 provides that information.

The distance of each of the 250 test observations was measured to these averages using the squared distance metric. Observation 251 was a 28-year-old applicant from Utah with a professional certification (no major) and 6 years experience (outcome minimal). First, the data

Table 6.11 Data conversion to 0–1 scale

Variable	Range	Value
Age	<20 20–50 >50	0 (Age-20)/30 1.0
State	CA Rest	1.0 0
Degree	Cert UG Rest	0 0.5 1.0
Major	IS Csci, Engr, Sci BusAd Other None	1.0 0.9 0.7 0.5 0
Experience	Max 1	Years/5

Table 6.12 Average transformed variable values for job applicant data

	Age	State	Degree	Major	Experience
Unacceptable	0.156322	0.137931	0.241379	0.186207	0.475862
Minimal	0.232068	0.303797	0.594937	0.517722	0.772152
Adequate	0.292346	0.237037	0.707407	0.833333	0.903704
Excellent	0.338095	0.285714	0.571429	0.985714	0.942857

needs to be transformed. Age 28 is 8 years above the minimum, yielding a transformed value of 0.267. The transformed state value is 0, transformed degree value is 0, and transformed major value is 0. Experience of 6 years transforms to a value of 1.0. The distance calculation is shown in Table 6.13.

The minimum sum of the squared distances was to the unacceptable group. Here, the minimum distance is to the unacceptable average. Table 6.14 shows the coincidence matrix for all 250 test cases.

This metric correctly classified 119 out of 250 chances, for a correct classification rate of 0.476. It was quite good at predicting the extreme cases.

Table 6.13 Calculation of squared distances

Average	Age	State	Degree	Major	Experience	Total
Unacceptable	$(0.267-0.156)^2$	$(0-0.138)^2$	$(0-0.241)^2$	$(0-0.186)^2$	$(1-0.476)^2$	
	0.012176	0.019025	0.058264	0.034673	0.274721	0.398859
Minimal	$(0.267-0.232)^2$	$(0-0.304)^2$	$(0-0.594)^2$	$(0-0.518)^2$	$(1-0.772)^2$	
	0.001197	0.092293	0.35395	0.268036	0.051915	0.76739
Adequate	$(0.267-0.292)^2$	$(0-0.237)^2$	$(0-0.707)^2$	$(0-0.833)^2$	$(1-0.904)^2$	
	0.000659	0.056187	0.500425	0.694444	0.009273	1.260989
Excellent	$(0.267-0.338)^2$	$(0-0.286)^2$	$(0-0.571)^2$	$(0-0.986)^2$	$(1-0.943)^2$	
	0.005102	0.081633	0.326531	0.971633	0.003265	1.388163

Table 6.14 Coincidence matrix for job applicant matching model using the squared error distance

Actual	Unacceptable	Minimal	Adequate	Excellent	Total
Unacceptable	19	5	6	0	30
Minimal	28	14	33	1	76
Adequate	2	16	73	37	128
Excellent	0	0	3	13	16
Total	49	35	115	51	250

R—*logistic*

We select the file LoanRaw400.csv in Figure 6.1. We deselect the intermediate variables Assets, Debts, and Want, which were used to generate
the risk rating. We unclick the Partition box because we are supplying a
test set. Then, click on the *Execute* tab.

R has the full slate of data mining algorithms, to include regression
models. They are attained under the *Model* tab as seen in Figure 6.2,
where you need to select the *Linear* button. Given that the data has a
categorical outcome, the *Logistic* button will automatically be selected.

Selecting *Execute* yields Figure 6.3.

The model for a logistic regression has β coefficients for continuous
variables, which are multiplied by variable values. For categorical variables,
the intercept contains the contribution for the case of amber credit and
high risk, which is adjusted if other categories are present. Significance is
as in linear regression. The calculation for the dependent variable is on a
logistic scale, which the software adjusts.

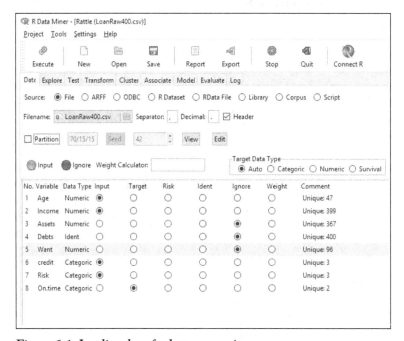

Figure 6.1 Loading data for loan regression

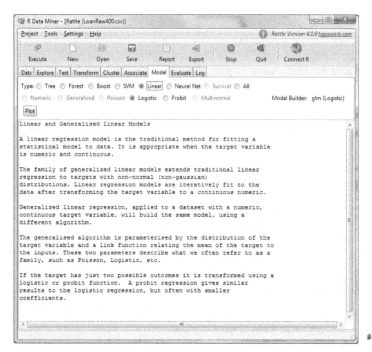

Figure 6.2 Model tab in R

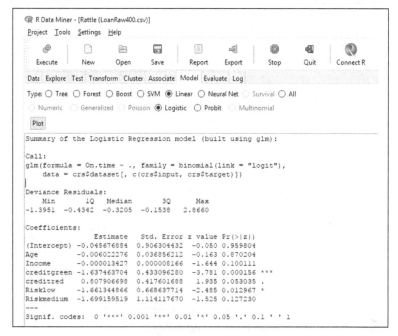

Figure 6.3 Logistic regression output for loan data from R

Evaluation of the model can be conducted by applying it to a test set (in our case 250 observations held out from the training set of 400—total dataset was 650). Figure 6.4 shows linking the test dataset. An alternative is to use Rattle's default by leaving the Partition box selected on the data page (70% training, 15% validation, 15% testing).

Click on the *Evaluate* tab, and select *CSV File*, which makes the *Document Link* tab available. Click on that search for the test file from your hard drive. *Execute* yields Table 6.15.

This coincidence matrix indicates an overall correct classification rate of 0.912 over the independent test set. The correct classification for OK cases was 0.926, while the correct classification for Problem cases was only 0.333. Thus, this model must be noted to be pretty bad at identifying Problem cases. The model can be applied to new cases if there is a file containing them. Figure 6.5 shows the Rattle screen. Note that you can select Class (for categorical prediction) or Probability (for continuous).

The Outcome column in this file can contain "?." Table 6.16 contains this data, with model predictions in probability form (0 is OK, 1 Fraud).

Applying the logistic regression model from R to this data resulted in classification of these cases, found the third and fourth rows predicted as problem loans, the rest OK.

Figure 6.4 Evaluation

Table 6.15 Coincidence matrix for R logistic regression model

	Predicted OK	Predicted problem	
Actual OK	226	4	230
Actual problem	18	2	20
	244	6	250

Figure 6.5 Rattle screen to apply model to new cases

Table 6.16 LoanRawNew.csv

Age	Income	Assets	Debts	Want	Credit	Risk	Outcome
55	75,000	80,605	90,507	3,000	Amber	High	0.200
30	23,506	22,300	18,506	2,200	Amber	Low	0.099
48	48,912	72,507	123,541	7,600	Red	High	0.454
22	8,106	0	1,205	800	Red	High	0.627
31	28,571	20,136	30,625	2,500	Amber	High	0.351
36	61,322	108,610	80,542	6,654	Green	Low	0.012
41	70,486	150,375	120,523	5,863	Green	Low	0.011
22	22,400	32,512	12,521	3,652	Green	Low	0.022
25	27,908	12,582	8,654	4,003	Amber	Medium	0.094
28	41,602	18,366	12,587	2,875	Green	Low	0.017

KNIME

A *File Reader* is used to link LoanRaw400.csv from the hard drive. This is *Configured* and *Executed*. A *Logistic Regression Learner* is dragged to the workflow and connected to the *File Reader*. In the *Configure* operation, the intermediate variables Assets, Debts, and Want are removed, as indicated in Figure 6.6.

Executing the Regression Learner yields Figure 6.7, the logistic regression model providing β coefficients as we obtained with R (although notably different).

We show the entire workflow for KNIME in Figure 6.8 to better explain the subsequent links and functions.

A *File Reader* in node 4 is used to link the test data (250 observations) from the hard drive. A *Regression Predictor* (node 3) is used to apply the model from *Logistic Regression Learner* to the test data. After the nodes are linked, and all *Executed*, the output is linked to a *Scorer* (node 5) to get a coincidence matrix, in this case, shown in Table 6.17.

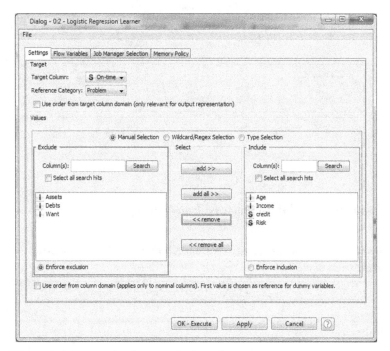

Figure 6.6 Regression learner for loan logistic regression

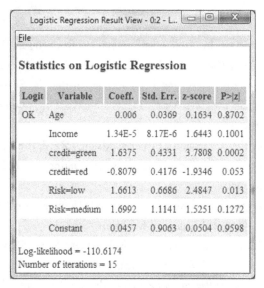

Figure 6.7 Logistic regression model from KNIME

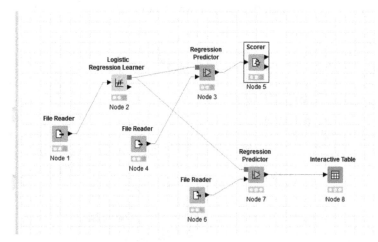

Figure 6.8 KNIME workflow for loan data

Table 6.17 Coincidence matrix from KNIME for the loan logistic regression model

	Predicted OK	Predicted problem	
Actual OK	224	6	230
Actual problem	17	3	20
	241	9	250

Row ID	⌄ Age	⌄ Income	⌄ Assets	⌄ Debts	⌄ Want	S credit	S Risk	S On-time	S Predict...
Row0	55	75000	80605	90507	3000	amber	high	OK	OK
Row1	30	23506	22300	18506	2200	amber	low	OK	OK
Row2	48	48912	72507	123541	7600	red	high	OK	OK
Row3	22	8106	0	1205	800	red	high	OK	Problem
Row4	31	28571	20136	30625	2500	amber	high	OK	OK
Row5	36	61322	108610	80542	6654	green	low	OK	OK
Row6	41	70486	150375	120523	5863	green	low	OK	OK
Row7	22	22400	32512	12521	3652	green	low	OK	OK
Row8	25	27908	12582	8654	4003	amber	medium	OK	OK
Row9	28	41602	18366	12587	2875	green	low	OK	OK

Figure 6.9 KNIME logistic regression loan new cases

Here, the relative accuracy is 227/250, the same 0.908 as obtained from the different logistic regression obtained with R. We add another *File Reader* to apply the model to 10 new cases (from file LoanRawNew. csv on the hard drive, which is linked to another *Regression Predictor* (node 7), which in turn is linked to an *Interactive Table* to predict the 10 new cases (shown in Figure 6.9).

In Figure 6.9, you can see that the KNIME logistic regression only predicted problems for case 4 (row3), as opposed to cases 3 and 4 from the R logistic regression.

WEKA

The same operation can be conducted with WEKA, beginning with opening the dataset (Figure 6.10). We use all 650 observations, as it is difficult to get WEKA to read test sets.

Here, we remove the intermediate variables Assets, Debts, and Want as we did with the other software. Modeling can be accomplished by selecting *Classify*, followed by *Functions*, and then *Logistic Regression* (only works with categorical output variable). This yields Figure 6.11.

We can use *Cross-validation* (10 fold is a good option), or a *Percentage split*. (In theory, you can use *Supplied test set*, but that is what WEKA has trouble reading). We choose 62 percent for the split to get close to what we used with R and KNIME. The model output is shown in Table 6.18.

Table 6.19 shows the resulting coincidence matrix.

This model actually has a slightly (very slightly) better fit than the R and KNIME models, with a 0.919 fit.

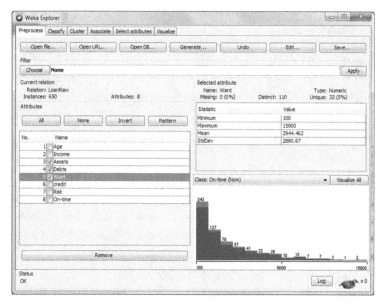

Figure 6.10 WEKA data loading for the loan dataset

Figure 6.11 WEKA logistic regression screen

Table 6.18 WEKA logistic regression model

Variable	Logistic coefficient
Age	−0.1407
Income	0
Credit=red	−1.1046
Credit=green	0.9042
Credit=amber	−0.4965
Risk=high	−0.7171

Risk=medium	0.3647
Risk=low	0.6593
Intercept	5.0063

Table 6.19 *Coincidence matrix from WEKA for loan logistic regression model*

	Predicted OK	Predicted problem	
Actual OK	227	1	228
Actual problem	19	0	19
	246	1	247

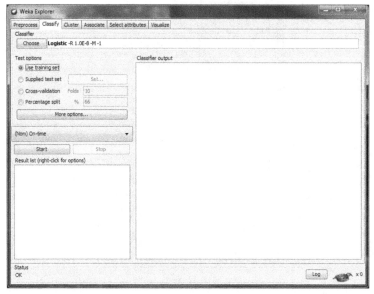

Figure 6.12 Logistic regression with WEKA—predicting new cases

To apply the model to new cases, you can add the new cases to the input data file. In this case, we added the 10 cases given in Table 6.16 to the LoanRaw.csv file, saving under the name LoanRawNew.csv. We read this into WEKA, as shown in Figure 6.12.

Note that we selected *Use training set.* Clicking on *More options ...,* we obtain the screen shown in Figure 6.13, and select *Output predictions.*

Then, the logistic regression model is run, as in Figure 6.14.

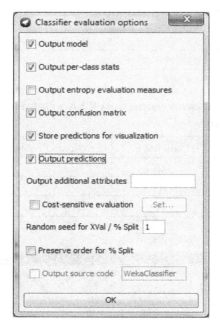

Figure 6.13 More options

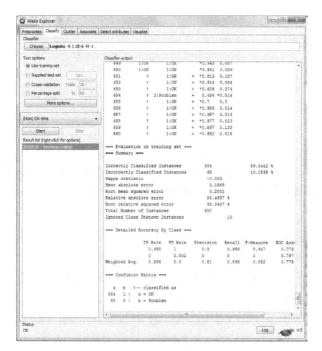

Figure 6.14 WEKA logistic regression for prediction

Figure 6.14 includes the full model, and a confusion matrix, but these are warped with the 10 new cases and are not the purpose of the output. Their purpose is to read the predictions, displayed (after 650 data points in the original full data set) as rows 651 through 660. The dataset had "?" values entered. The *Prediction* column shows that the fourth of these was categorized as a "Problem," the other nine as "OK." This matches the R logistic regression predictions.

Summary

Regression models have been widely used in classical modeling. They continue to be very useful in data mining environments, which differ primarily in the scale of observations and the number of variables used. Classical regression (usually OLS) can be applied to continuous data. If the output variables (or input variables) are categorical, logistic regression can be applied. Regression can also be applied to identify a discriminant function, separating observations into groups. If this is done, the cutoff limits to separate the observations based on the discriminant function score need to be identified. While discriminant analysis can be applied to multiple groups, it is much more complicated if there are more than two groups. Thus, other discriminant methods, such as the centroid method demonstrated in this chapter, are often used.

Regression can be applied by conventional software such as SAS, SPSS, or Excel. Additionally, there are many refinements to regression that can be accessed, such as stepwise linear regression. Stepwise regression uses partial correlations to select entering independent variables iteratively, providing some degree of automatic machine development of a regression model. Stepwise regression has its proponents and opponents, but is a form of machine learning.

CHAPTER 7

Neural Networks in Data Mining

As with many similar business data mining applications, the ability to predict customer success would make decision making a lot easier. While perfect prediction models cannot be expected, there are a number of data mining techniques that can improve the predictive ability. Neural network models are applied to data that can be analyzed by alternative models. The normal data mining process is to try all alternative models and see which works best for a specific type of data over time. But, there are some types of data where neural network models usually outperform the alternatives, such as regression or decision trees. Neural networks tend to work better when there are complicated relationships in the data, such as high degrees of nonlinearity. Thus, they tend to be viable models in problem domains where there are high levels of unpredictability. Commercial banking is one such area.

Neural networks can be applied to a variety of data types. One of the early applications of neural networks was in deciphering letters of the alphabet in character recognition. This involved 26 different letters, a finite number of outcomes, but much more than two. Many business prediction problems involve more than two outcomes, such as categories of employee performance. Often, however, two outcome categories will do nicely, such as on-time repayment or not. Neural networks can deal with both continuous data input and categorical data input, making them flexible models applicable to a number of data mining applications. The same is true for regression models and decision trees, all three of which support the data mining process of modeling.

Neural networks are the most widely used method in data mining. They are computer programs that take the previously observed cases to build a system of relationships within a network of nodes connected by arcs. Figure 7.1 gives a simple sketch of a neural network.

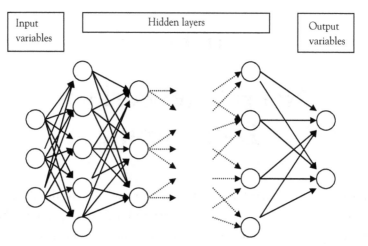

Figure 7.1 Simple neural network

The idea of neural networks came from the operation of neurons in the brain. Real neurons are connected to each other and accept electrical charges across synapses (small gaps between neurons), and in turn, pass on the electrical charge to other neighbor neurons. The relationship between real neural systems and artificial neural networks probably ends at that point. Human brains contain billions of synaptic connections, each of which contributes only a tiny bit to the overall transformation of the electrical synapses that encode knowledge.[1] This provides a tremendous amount of storage capacity and makes the loss of a few thousand synaptic connections (due to minor damage or cell death) immaterial. Artificial neural networks are usually arranged in at least three layers and have a defined and constant structure that is capable of reflecting complex nonlinear relationships, although they do not have anything near the capacity of the human brain. Each variable of input data (akin to the independent variables in regression analysis) have a node in the first layer. The last layer represents the output. For classification of the neural network models, this output layer has one node for each classification category (in the simplest case, output such as prediction of system success is either true or false). Neural networks almost always have at least one middle (hidden) layer of nodes that adds complexity to the model. (Two-layer neural networks have not proven to be very successful.)

Each node is connected by an arc to the nodes in the next layer. These arcs have weights, which are multiplied by the value of incoming nodes and summed. The input node values are determined by the variable values in the dataset. The middle-layer node values are the sum of the incoming node values multiplied by the arc weights. These middle node values, in turn, are multiplied by the outgoing arc weights to successor nodes. Neural networks "learn" through feedback loops. For a given input, the output for starting weights is calculated. The output is compared with target values, and the difference between the attained and target output is fed back to the system to adjust the weights on the arcs.

This process is repeated until the network correctly classifies the proportion of learning data specified by the user (tolerance level). Ultimately, a set of weights might be encountered that explains the learning (training) dataset very well. The better the fit that is specified, the longer the neural network will take to train, although there is really no way to accurately predict how long a specific model will take to learn. The resulting set of weights from a model that satisfies the set tolerance level is retained within the system for application to future data.

Neural Network Operation

These programs can be used to apply the learned experience to new cases, for decisions, classifications, and forecasts. Because they can take datasets with many inputs and relate them to a set of categorical outputs, they require little modeling. This is not to say that they are simply a black box into which the data miner can throw data and expect good output. Neural networks have relative advantages, in that they make no assumptions about the data properties or statistical distributions. They also tend to be more accurate when dealing with complex data patterns, such as nonlinear relationships.

There is modeling required when using neural networks in the sense of input variable selection, to include manipulation of input data as well as selection of neural network parameters, such as the number of hidden layers used. But, computer software can perform complex calculations, applying nonlinear regression to relate inputs to output.

There are many neural network models. About 95 percent of the business applications were reported to use *multilayered feedforward neural networks* with the *backpropagation* learning rule. This model supports the prediction and classification when fed inputs and known outputs. Back-propagation is a supervised learning technique, in that it uses a training set to fit relationships (or learn). This model uses one or more hidden layers of neurons between inputs and outputs. Each element in each layer is connected to all elements of the next layer, and each connecting arc has a weight, which is adjusted until the rate of explanation is at or above a prescribed level of accuracy. The hidden layers provide a means to reflect nonlinearities quite well relative to regression models. The neural network model is computationally intensive.

Many business applications do not have as much data as would be ideal. Neural network software products take over from this point. Back-propagation is a means to explore the vector space of its hidden nodes and to find the effective linear or nonlinear transformations. Philosophers in artificial intelligence view this feature as a potential means for artificial neural network models to learn, by identifying a complex set of weights that we never could have identified *a priori*.

While multilayered feedforward neural networks are analogous to regression and discriminant analysis in dealing with cases where training data is available, *self-organizing neural networks* are analogous to clustering techniques used, when there is no training data. The intent is to classify data to maximize the similarity of patterns within clusters while minimizing the similarity of patterns of different clusters. Kohonen self-organizing feature maps were developed to detect strong features of large datasets.[2]

Neural Networks in Data Mining

Artificial neural networks are the most common form of data mining models. They are extremely attractive because they can be fed data without a starting model estimation. This does not mean that they are best applied by automatically letting them operate on the data without model design. However, they are capable of going a long way toward the idea of the computer generating its own predictive model.

Neural network applications span most data mining activity, except for rule-based systems that are applied when the explanation of model results is emphasized, and the more exploratory data mining operations of market basket analysis. Neural networks have also been applied to stock market trading, electricity trading, and many other transactional environments. A common theme is to classify a new case for which multiple measures are available into a finite set of classes, such as on-time repayment, late repayment, or default.

Artificial neural networks operate much like regression models, except that they try many different β coefficient values to fit the training set of data until they obtain a fit as good as the modeler specifies. Artificial neural network models have the added benefit of considering variable interactions, giving them the ability to estimate training data contingent upon other independent variable values. (This could also be done with regression, but would lead to a tremendous amount of computational effort.)

Software Demonstration

We demonstrate open source software neural networks with the loan application dataset. The 650 observations in this dataset were divided; the first 400 observations were used for training and the model tested on the last 250 observations.

R (Rattle)

Data is loaded as we did with regression. We prune the data by selecting *Ignore* for intermediate variables, so Figure 7.2 matches Figure 6.1.

It is necessary to click on the *Execute* button to enact these choices. To run a neural network model, select the *Model* tab and click on the *Neural Net* radio button. This yields Figure 7.3.

Again, *Execute* needs to be clicked on. This yields Figure 7.4, and shows weights. The control for neural networks is the number of hidden layers.

Neural networks are black boxes in the sense that while in fact you could take the given weights and apply them, you don't want to because there are so many. The next step is to evaluate this model (built using 400

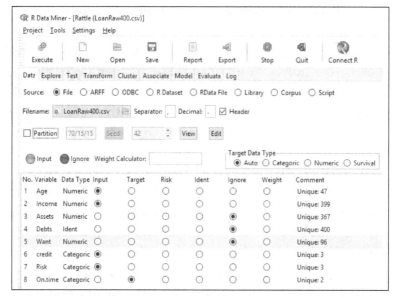

Figure 7.2 Rattle screen to select the loan data

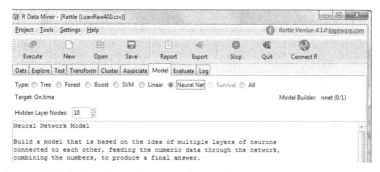

Figure 7.3 Rattle neural net opening screen

observations) on the test set of 250 observations. Select the *Evaluate* tab, as shown in Figure 7.5.

To obtain fit in the form of a coincidence (R calls it confusion) matrix, select the *CSV File* radio button, which allows you to link the test file. This yielded a degenerate model, calling all cases "OK." This is not a useful model. It often arises with unbalanced data (as we have here, where one outcome is predominant over the other). The cure is to either balance the data. (The easiest ways are to replicate the rare (Problem) cases in training data or delete some of the majority (OK here) or to change model parameters.) But, it is an advanced practice to figure out how to

Figure 7.4 R Neural network model for the loan data

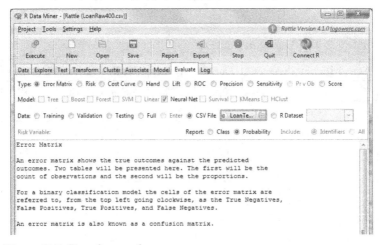

Figure 7.5 R evaluate tab

adjust R neural network parameters. When we raised the number of hidden nodes from 10 to 20 and reran, we still obtained a degenerate model. The number of hidden nodes is the only parameter Rattle provides for neural network models. To balance the training data, we replicated the 45 "Problem" cases 6 times, yielding a more balanced training set with 355 cases for both "OK" and 315 for "Problem." This yielded results as shown in Table 7.1.

This outcome has a correct classification rate of 0.756. To obtain forecasts for new cases, you can select the *Score* radio button and attach a file of new cases (here, we used file LoanRawNew.csv), which contained the data in Table 7.2.

These can be scored by R by selecting *Evaluate*, *Score*, and loading the CSV file with the data in Table 7.3, asking for a report of *Class*. Figure 7.6 shows how to do this.

This yielded the output in Table 7.3.

In this case, all 10 cases were categorized as "OK."

Table 7.1 *R neural net coincidence matrix*

	Model OK	Model problem	
Actual OK	177	53	230
Actual problem	8	12	20
	185	65	250

Table 7.2 *File LoanRawNew.csv*

Age	Income	Assets	Debts	Want	Credit	Risk	On-time
55	75,000	80,605	90,507	3,000	Amber	High	OK
30	23,506	22,300	18,506	2,200	Amber	Low	OK
48	48,912	72,507	123,541	7,600	Red	High	OK
22	8,106	0	1,205	800	Red	High	OK
31	28,571	20,136	30,625	2,500	Amber	High	OK
36	61,322	108,610	80,542	6,654	Green	Low	OK
41	70,486	150,375	120,523	5,863	Green	Low	OK
22	22,400	32,512	12,521	3,652	Green	Low	OK
25	27,908	12,582	8,654	4,003	Amber	Medium	OK
28	41,602	18,366	12,587	2,875	Green	Low	OK

Table 7.3 R Neural net classifications

Age	Income	Assets	Debts	Want	Credit	Risk	On-time	nnet
55	75,000	80,605	90,507	3,000	Amber	High	?	OK
30	23,506	22,300	18,506	2,200	Amber	Low	?	OK
48	48,912	72,507	123,541	7,600	Red	High	?	OK
22	8,106	0	1,205	800	Red	High	?	OK
31	28,571	20,136	30,625	2,500	Amber	High	?	OK
36	61,322	108,610	80,542	6,654	Green	Low	?	OK
41	70,486	150,375	120,523	5,863	Green	Low	?	OK
22	22,400	32,512	12,521	3,652	Green	Low	?	OK
25	27,908	12,582	8,654	4,003	Amber	Medium	?	OK
28	41,602	18,366	12,587	2,875	Green	Low	?	OK

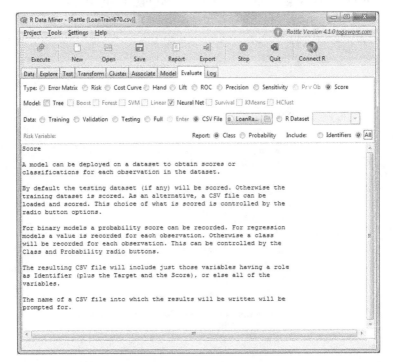

Figure 7.6 Selecting neural net classification in R

KNIME

KNIME has the feature that the workflow for other models can be modified to build other models. We can take the workflow from Figure 6.10 and replace the regression learner and predictor with neural network counterparts. Thus, the sequence is to load the training set with *Browse*, *Configure*, and *Execute*, yielding Figure 7.7.

KNIME has two neural network algorithms. RProp uses the multilayer feedforward networks. If the expected outcome is nominal, the output will be class assignment. If the data is not nominal, a regression value is computed. The PNN algorithm trains a probabilistic neural network using the dynamic decay adjustment method. This algorithm needs numeric data. The model output port contains the PNN model, which can be used for prediction in the PNN Predictor node. In our case, we have nominal output, so we need the RProp algorithm. The data for neural network analysis in KNIME needs to be normalized. We select the Normalizer (PMML) icon and drag it to the workflow. *Configure* and *Execute* yields Figure 7.8.

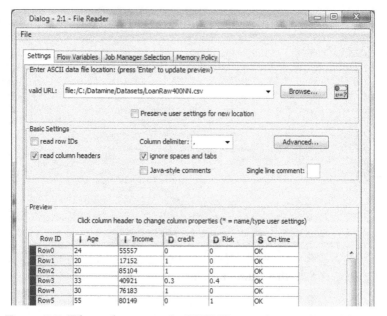

Figure 7.7 File reader output for KNIME neural network model

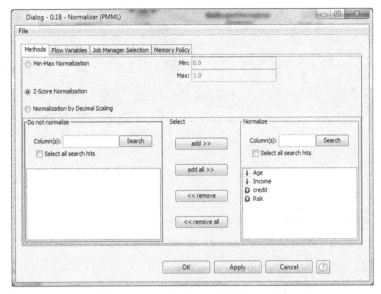

Figure 7.8 KNIME normalizer screen

The next operation is to drag in a PNN Learner node. *Configure* allows you to set the number of hidden layers and neurons. *Execute* runs the neural network model. We now want to test the model and bring in another File Reader node, which is linked to the file LoanTest250NN. We have to normalize this data in the same manner that we normalized the training file. *Executing* both files allows us to feed into a MultiLayerPerceptron Predictor node. *Executing* then can feed into a *Scorer* node. Figure 7.9 shows the workflow.

In *configuring* the Scorer node, make sure that the Script variables for On-time are selected. If you score a numerical model, you get 250 rows. With categorical On-time, you get a coincidence matrix. Unfortunately, in this case, the neural network yields a degenerate model. The RProp MLP Learner node can be used to specify more hidden layers and nodes, but it still generates a degenerate model. Thus, training data needs to be balanced and fed into node 1 of Figure 7.8. File LoanRaw670.csv includes extra 270 "Problem" outcomes by duplicating the original 45 "Problem" cases in the training set six times, resulting in 355 cases for both "OK" and "Problem." Going through the path from node 1 through node 15, this yields the coincidence matrix in Table 7.4.

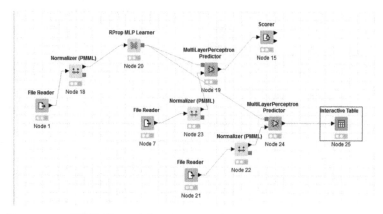

Figure 7.9 KNIME workflow for neural network model

Table 7.4 KNIME coincidence matrix

	Model OK	Model problem	
Actual OK	193	37	230
Actual problem	18	2	20
	211	39	250

Row ID	D Age	D Income	D credit	D Risk	S On-time	D P (On-ti...	D P (On-ti...	S Predicti...
Row0	1.901	1.52	-0.513	-1.081	OK			OK
Row1	-0.341	-0.767	-0.513	0.921	OK			Problem
Row2	1.273	0.361	-1.212	-1.081	OK			Problem
Row3	-1.058	-1.452	-1.212	-1.081	OK			Problem
Row4	-0.251	-0.542	-0.513	-1.081	OK			OK
Row5	0.197	0.912	1.119	0.921	OK			OK
Row6	0.646	1.32	1.119	0.921	OK			OK
Row7	-1.058	-0.817	1.119	0.921	OK			OK
Row8	-0.789	-0.572	-0.513	-0.28	OK			Problem
Row9	-0.52	0.036	1.119	0.921	OK			OK

Figure 7.10 KNIME neural network forecasts—New cases

This has a correct classification rate of 0.780. This model can be applied to new cases as with R. Figure 7.10 shows the output.

Figure 7.10 shows that four new cases are identified as potentially problematic. The graphic also includes a probabilistic assessment that amplifies the information content of the binary prediction. The variable values are numbers that were categorical, were given numerical values for neural network reading, then normalized by KNIME. (Note that the

On-Time "OK" list doesn't mean anything.) Low risk ratings seem to play a role in prediction, as does low income.

WEKA

Figure 7.11 shows the loading of the data file in WEKA.

To run a neural network model, select *Classify*, *Functions*, and *MultilayerPerceptron*. This yields Figure 7.12, which allows the user to change the parameters.

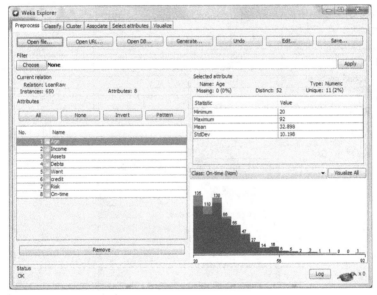

Figure 7.11 WEKA *opening screen*

Figure 7.12 WEKA *MultiLayerPerceptron display*

We use the defaults, with 10-fold cross-validation. This results in the coincidence matrix given in Table 7.5.

This model, thus, had a correct classification rate of 0.90, better than the other nondegenerate models. Degenerate models would have a correct classification rate of 0.92, but would provide no useful output. Applying this model would require appending the new cases to the bottom of the input file and going through the sequence: *More options ...*, obtaining Figure 7.13.

Table 7.5 *WEKA neural network coincidence matrix*

	Model OK	Model problem	
Actual OK	222	9	231
Actual problem	16	3	19
	238	12	250

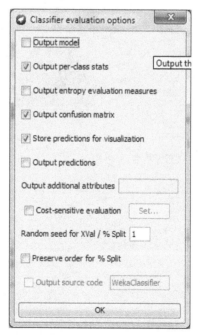

Figure 7.13 *WEKA process to obtain predictions*

We might consider 10 new cases, as shown in Table 7.6.

The premise is that we don't know the outcomes, but we need to enter something that was in the training set, so we arbitrarily enter "OK." To obtain predictions, select the radio button *Use training set*, select *More options …* and click on the *Output predictions* box and rerun the model. The resulting forecasts might be obtained as in Table 7.7.

Table 7.6 *New cases for WEKA*

Age	Income	Credit	Risk	Unknown outcome
55	75,000	Amber	High	OK
30	23,506	Amber	Low	OK
48	48,912	Red	High	OK
22	8,106	Red	High	OK
31	28,571	Amber	High	OK
36	61,322	Green	Low	OK
41	70,486	Green	Low	OK
22	22,400	Green	Low	OK
25	27,908	Amber	Medium	OK
28	41,602	Green	Low	OK

Table 7.7 *WEKA predictions for the loan data*

Instance	Phony actual	Predicted	Error	Probability distribution
651	1:OK	1:OK	*0.931	0.069
652	1:OK	1:OK	*0.828	0.172
653	1:OK	1:OK	*0.724	0.276
654	1:OK	1:OK	*0.582	0.418
655	1:OK	1:OK	*0.731	0.269
656	1:OK	1:OK	*0.991	0.009
657	1:OK	1:OK	*0.993	0.007
658	1:OK	1:OK	*0.976	0.024
659	1:OK	1:OK	*0.938	0.062
660	1:OK	1:OK	*0.985	0.01

Note that the model has a high propensity to call cases OK (like the model obtained from R).

Neural Network Products

Many data mining software products include neural network technology. This is a black box, in that much of the control is internal to the software, although some allow parameters, such as the number of layers, to be controlled by the user. There also are many neural network products listed on the Web. The site www.kdnuggets.com has a section on software, including a section on neural products. This dynamic market includes products free for download.

Summary

Regression models have been widely used in classical modeling. They continue to be very useful in data mining environments, which differ primarily in the scale of observations and the number of variables used. Neural networks have the very important strength that they can be applied to most data mining applications, and require minimal model building. They provide good results in complicated applications, especially when there are complex interactions among variables in the data. Neural networks can deal with categorical and continuous data. There also are many packages available.

There are some weaknesses of the method. The data needs to be massaged a bit, but that is not a major defect. The primary problem is that the neural network output tends to have a black-box effect, in that explanations in the form of a model are not available. Neural networks also have the technical defect of potentially converging to an inferior solution. However, this technical defect is detectable when applied to the test set of data.

Neural networks are, therefore, very attractive for problems where explanation of conclusions are not needed. This is often the case in classification and prediction problems. Neural networks should not be applied with excessive numbers of variables. Decision tree methods can be used to prune variables in that case. Genetic algorithms can also be applied to improve the neural network performance.

CHAPTER 8

Decision Tree Algorithms

Decision trees provide a means to obtain product-specific forecasting models in the form of rules that are easy to implement. These rules have an *if-then* form, which is easy for the users to implement. This data mining approach can be used by groceries in a number of policy decisions, to include ordering inventory replenishment, as well as evaluation of alternative promotion campaigns.

As was the case with regression models and neural networks, decision tree models support the data mining process of modeling. *Decision trees* in the context of data mining refer to the tree structure of rules (often referred to as association rules). The data mining decision tree process involves collecting those variables that the analyst thinks might bear on the decision at issue, and analyzing these variables for their ability to predict outcome. Decision trees are useful to gain further insights into customer behavior as well as lead to ways to profitably act on the results. The algorithm automatically determines which variables are the most important, based on their ability to sort the data into the correct output category. The method has relative advantage over neural networks and genetic algorithms, in that a reusable set of rules are provided, thus explaining model conclusions. There are many examples where decision trees have been applied to business data mining, including classifying loan applicants, screening potential consumers, and rating job applicants.

Decision trees provide a way to implement rule-based system approaches. The ID3 system selects an attribute as a root, with *branches* for different values of the attribute. All objects in the training set are classified into these branches. If all objects in a branch belong to the same output class, the *node* is labeled, and this branch is terminated. If there are multiple classes on a branch, another attribute is selected as a node, with all possible attribute values branched. An entropy *heuristic* is used to select the attributes with the highest information. In other data mining tools, other bases for selecting branches are often used.

Decision Tree Operation

A bank may have a database of past loan applicants for short-term loans. This database (a simplification of Table 4.4) consists of the age of the applicant, the applicant's income, and risk rating. The outcome of the loan is paid on time or not. The bank's policy treats the applicants differently by age group, income level, and risk. Age groups are less than or equal to 30, over 30 but less than or equal to 60, and over 60 years. Income levels are less than or equal to $30,000 per year, over $30,000 but less than or equal to $80,000 per year, and over $80,000 per year. High risk is defined as applicants with greater debt than assets. If an applicant's assets minus the requested loan amount exceed debt, the applicant is classified as low risk. Applicants with asset–debt relationships between these values are classified as medium risk. A tree sorts the possible combination of these variables. An exhaustive tree enumerates all combinations of variable values in Table 8.1.

Table 8.1 Enumeration of appliance loan variable combinations

Age = young	Income = low	Risk = low
		Risk = medium
		Risk = high
	Income = average	Risk = low
		Risk = medium
		Risk = high
	Income = high	Risk = low
		Risk = medium
		Risk = high
Age = middle	Income = low	Risk = low
		Risk = medium
		Risk = high
	Income = average	Risk = low
		Risk = medium
		Risk = high
	Income = high	Risk = low
		Risk = medium
		Risk = high

Age = old	Income = low	Risk = low Risk = medium Risk = high
	Income = average	Risk = low Risk = medium Risk = high
	Income = high	Risk = low Risk = medium Risk = high

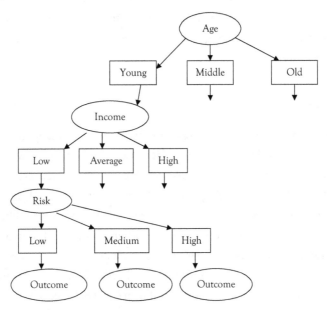

Figure 8.1 Partial tree for loan application data

The tree for this set of rules is partially shown in Figure 8.1.

A *rule-based system* model would require that the bank loan officers, who had respected judgment, be interviewed to classify (and justify) the decision for each of these combinations of variables. Some trees may be simplified. For instance, if income is high, the loan might be automatically granted by some loan officers. This would reduce the tree, as age and risk would not matter in that case. Further, for those without low income, if risk were high, the loan might not be granted. The first rule would be as shown in Table 8.2.

Table 8.2 Initial rule

Age	Income	Risk	Rule
	High		Grant loan
	Not high		Deny loan

This structure uses classification data, because there are a clear, finite number of outcomes (don't grant the loan, grant the loan, and possibly authorize part of the loan). This form of tree is referred to as a classification tree. Trees can also be used on data with continuous outcomes, in an estimating or predicting mode. In these cases, the terminology is a *regression tree*.

Rule Interestingness

Data, even categorical data, can involve potentially many rules. For instance, in the loan application data just presented, there were four variables, each of which could take on three values. There were 3 × 3 × 3 = 27 combinations, each given in Table 8.1. If there were 10 variables, each with 4 possible values, the number of combinations would be over a million (1,048,576). Clearly, brute force generation of rule outcomes is unreasonable. Fortunately, decision tree methods identify the most useful rules in terms of predicting outcomes. Rule effectiveness is measured in terms of confidence and support. Confidence is the degree of accuracy of a rule. Support is the degree to which the antecedent conditions occur in the data. Support for an association rule indicates the proportion of records covered by the set of attributes in the association rule. If there were 10 million book purchases, support for the given rule would be 10/10,000,000, a very small support measure of 0.000001. These concepts are often used in the form of threshold levels in machine learning systems. The minimum confidence levels and support levels can be specified to retain the rules identified by decision tree (or other association rule) methods.

For rules to be interesting, they must identify something useful (have a high confidence level and sufficiently high support) and novel. For instance, a grocer applying data mining finds that eggs and bacon are purchased together at a confidence level of 0.9 and a support level of 0.2 might not be impressed. The grocer knew that prior to data mining. Interestingness is the idea that the data mining analysis found out something that was unexpected (knowledge discovery). It is still useful to confirm the hypothesis that eggs and bacon sell together. But, it is more useful to discover the knowledge that blackberry jam and eggs go together at a similar rate. (Please note that we do not know of such a real relationship.) Such information could lead to rearrangement of store displays or promotions or both, which would make it interesting.

Machine Learning

Rule induction algorithms have been developed to automatically process data of this type. For this approach to work, a clear outcome is needed. In this case, a clear outcome exists—two categories of payoff results. Rule induction works by searching through data for patterns and relationships. The records can be clustered into specific categories. Machine learning starts with no assumptions—thus looking only at the input data and results. The judgment developed by human experts is not considered, which might sound inefficient, but human biases can, thus, be eliminated. Recursive partitioning algorithms split data (original data, not grouped as aforementioned) into finer and finer subsets, leading to a decision tree.

For instance, let us consider the 20 past loan application cases in Table 8.3, with known outcomes.

Table 8.3 Twenty past loan application cases

Age	Income	Assets	Debts	Want	Risk	Result
20 (young)	17,152 (low)	11,090	20,455	400	High	On-time
23 (young)	25,862 (low)	24,756	30,083	2,300	High	On-time
28 (young)	26,169 (low)	47,355	49,341	3,100	High	Late
23 (young)	21,117 (low)	21,242	30,278	300	High	Default
22 (young)	7,127 (low)	23,903	17,231	900	Low	On-time
26 (young)	42,083 (average)	35,726	41,421	300	High	Late
24 (young)	55,557 (average)	27,040	48,191	1,500	High	On-time
27 (young)	34,843 (average)	0	21,031	2,100	High	On-time

(*Continued*)

Table 8.3 Twenty past loan application cases (Continued)

Age	Income	Assets	Debts	Want	Risk	Result
29 (young)	74,295 (average)	88,827	100,599	100	High	On-time
23 (young)	38,887 (average)	6,260	33,635	9,400	Low	On-time
28 (young)	31,758 (average)	58,492	49,268	1,000	Low	On-time
25 (young)	80,180 (high)	31,696	69,529	1,000	High	Late
33 (middle)	40,921 (average)	91,111	90,076	2,900	Average	Late
36 (middle)	63,124 (average)	164,631	144,697	300	Low	On-time
39 (middle)	59,006 (average)	195,759	161,750	600	Low	On-time
39 (middle)	125,713 (high)	382,180	315,396	5,200	Low	On-time
55 (middle)	80,149 (high)	511,937	21,923	1,000	Low	On-time
62 (old)	101,291 (high)	783,164	23,052	1,800	Low	On-time
71 (old)	81,723 (high)	776,344	20,277	900	Low	On-time
63 (old)	99,522 (high)	783,491	24,643	200	Low	On-time

There are three variables, each with three possible levels. In practice, we would expect thousands of observations, making it unlikely that any combination would be empty. We use 20 observations to demonstrate the principals of the calculations. Of the 27 combinations, many here are empty. The combinations with representative observations are given in Table 8.4.

Automatic machine learning begins with identifying those variables that offer the greatest likelihood of distinguishing between the possible outcomes. For each of the three variables, we can identify the outcome probabilities in Table 8.5.

Most data mining packages use an *entropy* measure to gauge the discriminating power of each variable, selecting that variable with the greatest discriminating power as the first to split data with. (Chi-square measures can also be used to select variables.) There are three of the nine categories here with all observations in one outcome category or the other (age = old and risk = low, both have all cases in the on-time category; risk = average has only one observation, and it is in the late category—suspicious

Table 8.4 *Grouped data*

Age	Income	Risk	Total	On-time	Not on-time	Probability
Young	Low	High	4	2	2	0.50
Young	Low	Low	1	1	0	1.00
Young	Average	High	4	3	1	0.75
Young	Average	Low	2	2	0	1.00
Young	High	High	1	0	1	0.00
Middle	Average	Average	1	0	1	0.00
Middle	Average	Low	2	2	0	1.00
Middle	High	Low	2	2	0	1.00
Old	High	Low	3	3	0	1.00

Table 8.5 *Combination outcomes*

Variable	Value	Cases	On-time	Late	Prob (on-time)
Age	Young	12	8	4	0.67
	Middle	5	4	1	0.80
	Old	3	3	0	1.00
Income	Low	5	3	2	0.60
	Average	9	7	2	0.78
	High	6	5	1	0.83
Risk	High	9	5	4	0.55
	Average	1	0	1	0.00
	Low	10	10	0	1.00

logically and based on the minimum possible sample size, but remember, we are trying to demonstrate the procedure with a small dataset).

One formula for entropy where p is the number of positive examples and n is the number of negative examples in the training set for each value of the attribute is as follows:

$$\text{Information} = -\frac{p}{p+n}\log_2\frac{p}{p+n} - \frac{n}{p+n}\log_2\frac{n}{p+n}$$

This formula has a problem: if either p or n is 0 (which would happen if there were unanimous outcomes for a category), then the log to base 2 is undefined, and the formula does not work. However, for values just above 0, the Inform formula will converge to 0. For the variable Age, there are 3 outcomes. Entropy for each Age category by this formula is shown in Table 8.6.

For category Young, the calculation is [−(8/12) × (−0.585) − (4/12) × (−1.585)] × (12/20) = 0.551.

The lower this entropy measure, the greater the information content (the greater the agreement probability). The entropy measures for the three variables are:

Age	0.731
Income	0.782
Risk	0.446

By this measure, Risk has the greatest information content. If Risk is low, the data indicates a 1.0 probability (10 of 10 cases) that the applicant will pay the loan back on-time. If Risk is not low, this data indicates a 0.5 probability that the applicant will pay the loan back on time. This would be the first rule selected by the machine learning algorithm.

IF (Risk = Low)	THEN Predict On-time payment
ELSE	Predict Late

This rule is subject to two types of errors. First, those applicants rated as low risk may actually not pay on time. (From the data, the probability of this happening is 0.0.) Second, those applicants rated as high or average risk may actually have paid if given a loan. (From the data, the probability of this happening is 0.5.) The expectation of this is the probability of an applicant being rated as high or average in risk (10/20, or 0.5) times the probability of being wrong (0.5), yielding an expected error of 0.25. To test this rule, it is best to apply it to a second set of data, different from the dataset used to develop the rule.

The set of rules can be examined further to see if greater accuracy can be obtained. The entropy formula for Age, given that risk was not low, is 0.991, while the same calculation for income is 1.971. This indicates that Age has greater discriminating power. With this data, if Age is middle,

Table 8.6 *Entropy calculation for Age*

	p/(p+n)	Log(base 2)	n/(p+n)	Log(base 2)	Sum of products	Probability (young)	Product
Young	8/12	-0.585	4/12	-1.585	0.918	12/20	0.551
Middle	4/5	-0.322	1/5	-2.322	0.722	5/20	0.180
Old	3/3	0*	0/3	0*	0*	3/20	0*
Sum							0.731

*formula strictly undefined, but converges to zero.

the one case did not pay on time. There were no old cases in this group. Therefore, the second rule is:

| IF (Risk is NOT low) | AND (Age = Middle) | THEN Predict Late |
| ELSE | | Predict On-time |

In this case, the data would indicate probabilities shown in Table 8.7.

All 10 of this subset of the data with Low risk rating paid on time. Of the other 10 cases that were not low, the 1 that was middle aged did not pay on time (as stated earlier), while 5 of the 9 young cases paid on time. The expected error here is the 4/9 probability for the 9 cases out of 20 total, or 0.2. This is an improvement over the prior case where the expected error was 0.25.

For the last variable, Income, given that Risk was not low, and Age was not Middle, there are nine cases left, shown in Table 8.8.

Four of these nine cases were Low income, with two paying on time and two not. Four were Average income, three of which paid on time and one not. The last case was High income, which was not paid on time.

A third rule, taking advantage of the case with unanimous outcome, is:

| IF (Risk NOT low) | AND (Age NOT middle) | AND (Income high) | THEN predict Late |
| ELSE | | | Predict on-time |

Table 8.7 Probabilities by case

Risk	Age	Count	Probability on-time
Low		10/20	1.0
NOT low	Middle	1/20	0.0
NOT low	Young	9/20	0.56

Table 8.8 Probabilities recalculated

Income	On-time	Late	Probability on-time
Low	2	2	0.50
Average	3	1	0.75
High	0	1	0.00

The expected accuracy of the three rules together is shown in Table 8.9. The expected error here is 8/20 times 0.375 = 0.15.

An additional rule could be generated. For the case of Risk NOT low, Age = Young, and Income NOT high, there are 4 cases with low income (probability of on-time = 0.5) and 4 cases with average income (probability of on-time = 0.75). The greater discrimination is provided by average income, resulting in the rule:

IF (Risk NOT low)	AND (Age NOT middle)	AND (Income average)	THEN predict on-time
ELSE			Predict either

There is no added accuracy obtained with this rule, shown in Table 8.10.

The expected error is 4/20 times 0.25 + 4/20 times 0.5, equals 0.15, the same as without the rule. When machine learning methods encounter no improvement, they generally stop. (Here, we have exhausted all combinations anyway.) Therefore, the last rule would *not* be added to the first three. The machine learning algorithm would stop at:

IF (Risk low)			THEN predict On-time
ELSE			
IF (Risk NOT low)	AND (Age middle)		THEN predict Late
ELSE			
IF (Risk NOT low)	AND (Age NOT middle)	AND (Income high)	THEN predict Late
ELSE			Predict On-time

Table 8.9 *Expected accuracy of three rules*

Risk	Age	Income	Count	Probability (on-time)
Low			10/20	1.0
NOT low	Middle		1/20	0.0
NOT low	Young	High	1/20	0.0
NOT low	Young	NOT high	8/20	0.625

This model can be tested with the data given in Table 8.5. Table 8.11 shows the results.

Figure 8.2 shows the decision tree for this set of rules.

In this case, the coincidence matrix is shown in Table 8.12.

Table 8.10 Accuracy of fourth rule

Risk	Age	Income	Count	Probability (on-time)
Low			10/20	1.0
NOT low	Middle		1/20	0.0
NOT low	Young	High	1/20	0.0
NOT low	Young	Average	4/20	0.75
NOT low	Young	Low	4/20	0.50

Table 8.11 Rules applied to test cases

Record	Actual	Rule prediction	By rule	Result
1	On-time	On-time	1	Match
2	On-time	On-time	1	Match
3	On-time	On-time	1	Match
4	On-time	On-time	Else	Match
5	On-time	On-time	1	Match
6	On-time	On-time	Else	Match
7	Late	On-time	Else	Miss
8	On-time	On-time	1	Match
9	On-time	Late	3	Miss
10	On-time	On-time	1	Match

Table 8.12 Coincidence matrix for rule set

Actual	Late	On-time	Total
Late	0	1	1
On-Time	1	8	9
Total	1	9	10

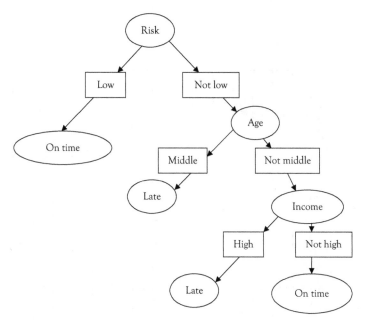

Figure 8.2 Decision tree for rule

In this case, the accuracy of the model is 8/10, or 80 percent. There were errors of both types (denying a good loan application, accepting one bad application).

Software Demonstrations

We use the loan application dataset to demonstrate the decision tree operation, both manually as well as with software. The full loan application dataset had 650 observations over 4 variables. We can use the first 400 observations for training, reserving the last 250 observations for testing. The data for this covered in Chapter 4 is grouped in Table 8.13.

Table 8.14 gives the categorical counts for middle-aged loan applicants. Finally, we have the Old applicants in Table 8.15.

Most of the possible old categories were vacant. Furthermore, all of the old applicant categories had unanimity in the outcome. Automatic machine learning begins with identifying those variables that offer the greatest likelihood of distinguishing between the possible outcomes. For each of the four variables, we can identify the outcome probabilities in Table 8.16.

Table 8.13 Grouped data—young

Age	Income	Risk	Credit rating	On-time	Not on-time	Probability
Young	Low	High	Red	3	1	0.750
			Amber	7	1	0.875
			Green	17	1	0.944
		Average	Red	1	1	0.500
			Green	1	0	1.000
		Low	Green	7	0	1.000
	Average	High	Red	9	9	0.500
			Amber	24	10	0.706
			Green	42	6	0.875
		Average	Amber	1	0	1.000
			Green	4	0	1.000
		Low	Red	2	0	1.000
	High	High	Red	1	1	0.500
			Amber	5	3	0.625
			Green	12	0	1.000

Table 8.14 Grouped data—middle aged

Age	Income	Risk	Credit rating	On-time	Not on-time	Probability
Middle	Low	Average	Green	3	0	1.000
		Low	Red	0	1	0
			Amber	1	0	1.000
	Average		Green	2	0	1.000
		High	Red	1	1	0.500
			Amber	4	2	0.667
			Green	17	1	0.944
		Average	Amber	4	0	1.000
			Green	4	0	1.000
		Low	Red	13	1	0.929
			Amber	37	4	0.902
			Green	64	1	0.985
	High	High	Amber	1	0	1.000
			Green	7	0	1.000
		Low	Red	8	0	1.000
			Amber	14	0	1.000
			Green	30	0	1.000

Table 8.15 Grouped data—age equals old

Age	Income	Risk	Credit rating	On-time	Not on-time	Probability
Old	Average	Low	Red	0	1	0
			Amber	1	0	1.000
			Green	2	0	1.000
	High	Low	Red	2	0	1.000
			Amber	1	0	1.000
			Green	3	0	1.000

Table 8.16 Combination outcomes

Variable	Value	Cases	On-time	Late	Prob (on-time)
Age	Young	169	136	33	0.805
	Middle	221	210	11	0.950
	Old	10	9	1	0.900
Income	Low	47	42	5	0.894
	Average	265	229	36	0.864
	High	88	84	4	0.955
Risk	High	186	150	36	0.806
	Average	19	18	1	0.947
	Low	195	187	8	0.959
Credit rating	Red	56	40	16	0.714
	Amber	120	100	20	0.833
	Green	224	215	9	0.960

For the variable Age, there are three outcomes. Entropy for Age by this formula would be as shown in Table 8.17.

Under the heading *Sum* is the following calculation. For Young, the first term of the Inform equation multiplies the ratio 136/169 times −0.313, and by −1. The second term multiplies the ratio 33/169 times −4.328, and by −1. The sum of these terms is 0.712. This represents 169 of the 400 training cases. The heading *Product* is the product of sum by probability. For Young, this is 0.712 times 169/400, yielding 0.301. The sum of the three products yields the entropy measure. The lower

Table 8.17 *Entropy calculation for Age*

	p/(p+n)	Log(base 2)	n/(p+n)	Log(base 2)	Sum	Probability	Product
Young	136/169	-0.313	33/169	-2.356	0.712	169/400	0.301
Middle	210/221	-0.074	11/221	-4.328	0.285	221/400	0.158
Old	9/10	-0.152	1/10	-3.322	0.469	10/400	0.012
Sum							**0.470**

this entropy measure, the greater the information content (the greater the agreement probability). The entropy measures for the four variables are:

Age	0.473
Income	0.500
Risk	0.470
Credit rating	0.461

By this measure, Credit rating has the greatest information content. Among the Credit rating categories, we want to select that one with the greatest ability to accurately categorize data (the closest probability to 1.0 for Loan, or 0.0 for Deny Loan). We can consider the relative cost of an error. An error of granting a loan to a case where it is not paid on time may cost nine times ($900) as much as one that does pay on time (but was denied, $100). We can, therefore, use a cutoff limit of 0.90 probability. If the category being considered has a probability greater than or equal to 0.9, we will create a rule granting the loan. If the category being considered has a probability less than 0.9, we will deny the loan. If Credit rating is green, the data indicates a 0.953 probability (244 of 256 cases) that the applicant will pay the loan back on time. If Credit rating is not green, this data indicates a 0.815 probability that the applicant will pay the loan back on time. This would be the first rule selected by the machine learning algorithm.

IF (Credit = Green)	THEN Predict On-time Payment
ELSE	Predict Late

This rule is subject to two types of errors. First, those applicants rated as green may actually not pay on time. (From the data, the probability of this happening is 0.040). Second, those applicants rated as amber or red may actually have paid, if given a loan. (From the data, the probability of this happening is 0.815). The expectation of this is the probability of an applicant being rated as green (224/400, or 0.550) times the probability of being wrong (0.040), plus the probability of not being green (176/400, or 0.440) times the probability of being wrong (0.795), yielding an expected error of 0.022 + 0.350 = 0.372. We can also calculate the error cost function. This would be $900 times 0.022 + $100 times

0.350, or $55.14. To test this rule, it is best to apply it to a second set of data, different from the dataset used to develop the rule. Using the last 250 observations as the test set, Table 8.18 shows the coincidence matrix.

The correct classification rate was 0.620. The cost function for this result would be $900 times 7 plus $100 times 88, or $15,100. Since we had 250 cases, the average error cost would have been $60.40 per case.

The set of rules can be examined further to see if greater accuracy can be obtained. The entropy formula for Age, given that Credit rating was not green, is 0.672, for Income 0.720, for Risk 0.657, and for the difference between red and amber Credit rating is 0.718. This indicates that Risk has the greater discriminating power at this point. With this data, if Risk is low, 79 of the 86 cases paid on time (0.919). The other two states had 61 of 90 pay on time (0.678). Therefore, the second rule is:

IF (Credit Rating is NOT green)	AND (Risk = Low)	THEN Predict On-Time
ELSE		Predict Late

In this case, the data would indicate probabilities shown in Table 8.19.

The expected error here is the 224/400 times (1 − 0.960) + 86/400 times (1 − 0.919) + 90/400 times (1 − 0.678), or 0.112. The cost function is $900 times 224/400 times 0.040 ($20.16) plus $900 times 86/400 times 0.081 ($15.67) plus $100 times 90/400 times 0.678 ($15.26), or $51.09 per case. This is an improvement over the prior case where the

Table 8.18 *Coincidence matrix for first rule*

Actual	Late	On-time	Total
Late	13	7	20
On-time	88	142	230
Total	101	149	250

Table 8.19 *Probabilities by case*

Credit rating	Risk	Count	Probability on-time
Green		224/400	0.960
NOT green	Low	86/400	0.919
NOT green	NOT low	90/400	0.678

expected error was 0.380 with an expected cost per case of $60.40. The coincidence matrix is as shown in Table 8.20.

The correct classification rate was 0.792, much better than in Table 8.18. The cost function here would be $900 times 9 plus $100 times 43, or $12,400, or $49.60 per case.

We recalculate entropy, eliminating Credit rating green and Risk rating Low. The values obtained were 0.902 for Age, 0.893 for Income, 0.897 for Risk, and 0.877 for Credit rating. The lowest of these values was for Credit. Given that Credit rating was not green and Risk was not high, there are 90 training cases left, shown in Table 8.21.

While below the specified cutoff limit of 0.9, those with Amber credit ratings clearly had a higher probability of on-time payment than did those with credit ratings of red. A third rule is:

IF (Credit Rating NOT green)	AND (Risk NOT high)	AND (Credit Rating amber)	THEN predict On-Time
ELSE			Predict Late

The expected accuracy of the three rules together is shown in Table 8.22.

The expected error here is 0.117, with an expected cost function per case of $75.57 (due to the high error rate for the third rule). The expected classification error went down, although the expected cost function went

Table 8.20 Coincidence matrix for first two rules

Actual	Late	On-time	Total
Late	11	9	20
On-time	43	187	230
Total	54	196	250

Table 8.21 Probabilities recalculated

Credit Rating	On-time	Late	Probability on-time
Red	15	13	0.536
Amber	46	16	0.742

Table 8.22 *Expected accuracy of three rules*

Credit rating	Risk	Credit rating	Count	Probability (on-time}
Green			224/400	0.960
NOT green	High		86/400	0.919
NOT green	NOT high	Amber	62/400	0.742
NOT green	NOT high	NOT high	28/400	0.536

Table 8.23 *Coincidence matrix for three rules*

Actual	Late	On-time	Total
Late	3	17	20
On-time	11	219	230
Total	14	236	250

up. Table 8.23 gives the coincidence matrix for this set of rules using the test data.

Here, the correct classification rate increased to 0.888 (it was 0.792 after two rules), while the average cost per case increased to $65.60 from $49.60. When machine learning methods encounter no improvement, they generally stop. Therefore, the last rule would *not* be added to the first two. The machine learning algorithm would stop at:

IF (Credit Rating is green)		THEN Predict On-time
IF (Credit Rating is NOT green)	AND (Risk = Low)	THEN Predict On-time
ELSE		Predict Late

Note that this approach does not guarantee optimality. In that sense, it is heuristic, which means it tends to give good models, but there might be better ones.

The model was also run using See 5, a very good decision tree software. The initial model, using 400 training observations of categorical, degenerated to classifying all cases as On-Time. Due to the highly skewed dataset (where 45 cases were late and 355 were on-time), this had a fairly high correct classification rate of 0.920. However, it was very bad at predicting applications that would end up late. Balancing the data can improve

Table 8.24 Results from the balancing dataset

Train set	Late	On-time	Proportion	Predict 0 = 1	Predict 1 = 0	Correct rate	Cost
400	45	355	0.1125	20	0	0.920	$18,000
325	45	280	0.1385	20	0	0.920	$18,000
225	45	180	0.2000	9	39	0.808	$12,000
180	45	135	0.2500	9	39	0.808	$12,000
150	45	105	0.3000	9	32	0.956	$11,300

results. We pruned the observations from the training set to control the proportion of late cases, as shown in Table 8.24. Using 325 observations again yielded all forecasts to be on time. The model based on 225 observations (as well as the model based on 180 observations) was to classify all cases as on-time unless risk was high, and credit was either red or amber. The model using 150 training cases was to classify all cases as on-time unless the applicant was young and credit was either red or amber. The models obtained were tested on the same test set of 250 observations.

This data shows a clear trend toward more useful model results by balancing data.

R Decision Tree Model

We now demonstrate decision trees on the loan application dataset with R (Rattle). Figure 8.3 shows the modeling screen from Rattle for decision trees (the *Tree* radio button is the default).

Figure 8.4 shows the rules obtained from *Execute* being selected in Figure 8.3.

This tree has six rules (the asterisked lines in Figure 8.4). Selecting the *Draw* button on Figure 8.4 yields the graphic tree in Figure 8.5.

Table 8.25 gives the coincidence matrix for this decision tree.

Correct classification here is 0.880, quite good. For the actual "OK" cases, the correct classification rate is 219/230 = 0.952, while for the actual "Problem" cases, it is only 3/20, or 0.15. This model categorized case 4 as fraudulent, all others as "OK."

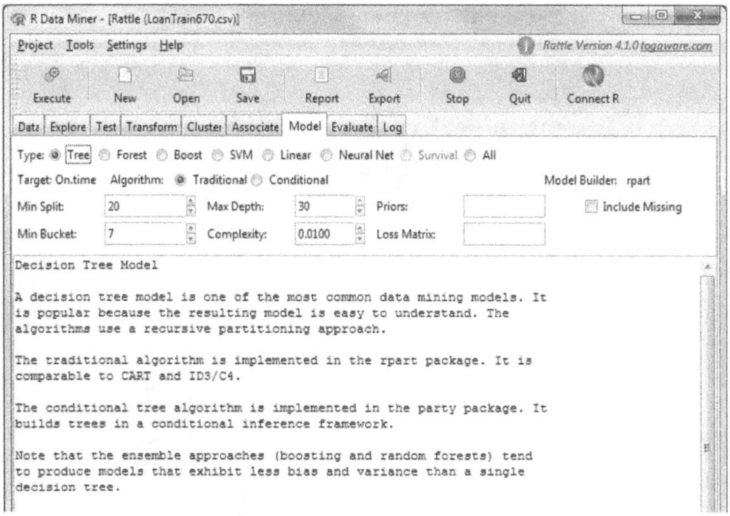

Figure 8.3 Opening Rattle decision tree screen

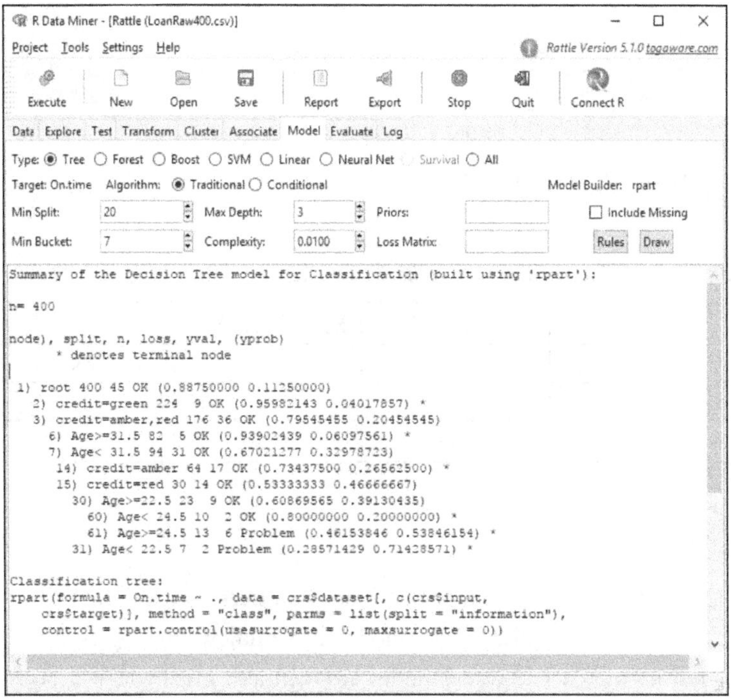

Figure 8.4 Rattle decision tree model for loan training file

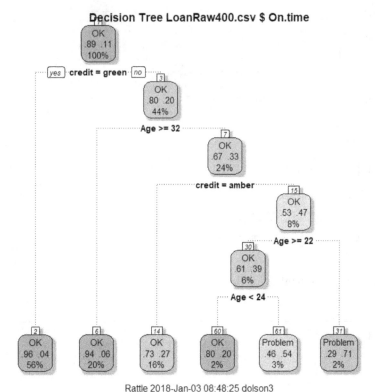

Figure 8.5 R decision tree

Table 8.25 Coincidence matrix for Rattle decision tree model

	Model OK	Model problem	
Actual OK	219	11	230
Actual problem	17	3	20
	236	14	250

KNIME

Figure 8.6 displays the workflow for decision trees using KNIME.

This is very similar to the modeling workflows for regression and neural networks. File reader nodes are identical. Here you will need a Decision Tree Learner node (node 2) and Decision Tree Predictor nodes (nodes 4 and 8). The scorer is the same. To forecast new cases, the new cases are input on the File Reader node 11, run through the Predictor in

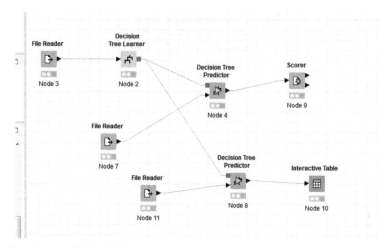

Figure 8.6 KNIME decision tree workflow

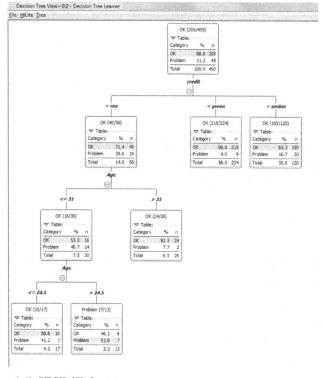

Figure 8.7 KNIME decision tree

node 8, and an Interactive Table attached in node 10. Figure 8.7 shows the resulting tree from the Decision Tree Learner.

Table 8.26 Coincidence matrix for Rattle decision tree model

	Model OK	Model problem	
Actual OK	221	9	230
Actual problem	19	1	20
	240	10	250

Row ID	Age	Income	Assets	Debts	Want	$ credit	$ Risk	$ On-time	$ Predicti...
Row0	55	75000	80605	90507	3000	amber	high	OK	OK
Row1	30	23506	22300	18506	2200	amber	low	OK	OK
Row2	48	48912	72507	123541	7600	red	high	OK	OK
Row3	22	8106	0	1205	800	red	high	OK	OK
Row4	31	28571	20136	30625	2500	amber	high	OK	OK
Row5	36	61322	108610	80542	6654	green	low	OK	OK
Row6	41	70486	150375	120523	5863	green	low	OK	OK
Row7	22	22400	32512	12521	3652	green	low	OK	OK
Row8	25	27908	12582	8654	4003	amber	medium	OK	OK
Row9	28	41602	18366	12587	2875	green	low	OK	OK

Figure 8.8 KNIME decision tree new case predictions

Note that the decision tree from Figure 8.7 classifies all 10 new cases as "OK."

The output from KNIME's Scorer node is given in Table 8.26.

Here the correct classification rate is 222/250, or 0.888 (slightly better than R's). The decision tree from KNIME was very good at predicting the actual "OK" cases (221/230, or 0.961), but not very good at predicting the "Problem" cases (1/20 = 0.05). The prediction of new cases is obtained from the Interactive Table node (see Figure 8.8).

WEKA

WEKA is opened as usual, and under *Preprocess*, the file with all 650 cases (training and test in Rattle and KNIME) linked. We selected 61.5 percent of the cases for training. J48 was run with minimum support of 2 yielded a degenerate model, as did minimum support of 20. Thus, we balanced the dataset by replicating the smaller "Problem" cases 8 times, yielding a balanced dataset with 585 cases for both "OK" and "Problem." We ran J48 decision tree model using 50 percent of this balanced data for testing. With minimum support of 2, the model contained 49 rules—too many rules. This model did have an overall correct classification rate of

0.911 which is actually very good, but a 0 correct rate of predicting the negatives. Raising minimum support to 20 yielded 21 rules and a correct classification rate of 0.802 (0.725 for positives, 0.879 for negatives). This is still too many rules, so minimum support was raised to 50.

These eight rules (Figure 8.9) yielded the coincidence matrix in Table 8.27.

The correct classification rate for positive cases was 0.752, for negative cases 0.750, and 0.751 overall. A nice feature of decision tree models is that they are easy to apply to new cases. They consist of *If/Then* rules that are very easy to interpret. By adjusting minimum support, you can balance the tradeoff between accuracy and smaller rule sets.

As to new cases, this model classified "Problem" for case in row 1 (see Figure 8.8 for input data) by rule 7, case in row 3 by rule 1, case in row 4 by rule 7, case in row 8 by rule 7, and case in row 9 by rule 3. Thus, this was a much more thorough (and probably useful) model than those decision tree models obtained from R and KNIME in this case.

```
Age <= 31
|   credit = red: Problem (181.0/28.0)                  Rule 1
|   credit = green
|   |   Income <= 34621: OK (65.0/9.0)                  Rule 2
|   |   Income > 34621
|   |   |   Age <= 28
|   |   |   |   Income <= 40285: Problem (50.0/14.0)    Rule 3
|   |   |   |   Income > 40285
|   |   |   |   |   Age <= 24: OK (51.0/18.0)           Rule 4
|   |   |   |   |   Age > 24: Problem (68.0/32.0)       Rule 5
|   |   |   Age > 28: OK (70.0/18.0)                    Rule 6
|   credit = amber: Problem (311.0/77.0)               Rule 7
Age > 31: OK (374.0/81.0)                               Rule 8
```

Figure 8.9 WEKA rules

Table 8.27 WEKA decision tree coincidence matrix

	Model OK	Model problem	
Actual OK	440	145	585
Actual problem	146	439	585
	586	584	1170

Summary

Decision trees are very effective and useful data mining models. They are automatic, an application of machine learning, which in itself makes them attractive. They are relatively robust, in that they are not adversely affected by noisy data or missing data. They can handle very large datasets and can deal with data in the categorical or numeric form. They are also very strong in their ability to explain their conclusions (rules can be expressed in natural language, and communication to managers is excellent). As shown in the preceding section, there are many software products available to support decision tree modeling.

CHAPTER 9

Scalability

Previous chapters have focused on explaining models. A small dataset (involving loan application approval) was used for demonstration. Data mining, and especially big data, implies much larger datasets. Real-time data collection of key data is going to occur for all of the typical datasets we have presented. The major difference in operations is in scalability. R works with massive datasets and is completely scalable. KNIME and WEKA are potentially limited in the ability to deal with large sets of data.

In this chapter, we will demonstrate some data characteristics with R. The data mining process presented in Chapter 3 needs to consider the outcome (some data is predictive, like the proportion of income expended on groceries or any other category of spending), yielding a continuous number. Many data mining applications call for classification (fraud or not; repayment expected or not; high, medium, or low performance). In both cases, the usual process is to try all three of the major predictive models (regression, neural networks, and decision trees). We will show the different data needs for each model for both the prediction and classification.

Another data issue is balance. In classification models, sometimes one outcome is much rarer than the other. One hopes that the incidence of cancer is very low, just as insurance companies hope that file claims will not be fraudulent, and bankers hope that loans will be repaid. When high degrees of imbalance are present, there is a propensity for algorithms to spit out models that simply say the majority class will always be the outcome. That yields a correct classification rate equal to the proportion of the majority outcome, which may exceed 0.99. But, this does not provide a useful classification model.

Balancing was described in the fraud data set. Essentially, there are two easy ways to balance data. (There are more involved methods, but they are essentially variants of these two easy approaches.) One is to delete excessive majority cases, but this is problematic, in that you need to be fair in selecting the cases selected for deletion. The other approach is to increase the minority cases. You need advanced approaches if you want a precise number of cases for each outcome. But, it is pretty simple to simply replicate all of the minority cases as many times as you need in order to obtain roughly the same number of cases for each category.

This chapter will demonstrate Rattle models for a bigger dataset. Expenditure data was described in earlier chapters and poses a situation where the objective is to predict the proportion of expendable income spent on a particular category, such as expenditure on automotives. As stated earlier, we will demonstrate regression, neural networks, and decision trees for both predictive and categorical data.

Expenditure Data

The dataset we will use has 10,000 observations, by no means massive, but a bit larger than the loan data we have used in prior chapters to demonstrate concepts. Expenditure data was described in Chapter 4. Here, we will begin by dividing the data into a training set of 8,000 observations and a test set of 2,000 observations. We also have a small set of 20 new cases for predictive purposes, as given in Table 9.1.

R (Rattle) Calculations

We took the original data and made it binary by assigning the continuous variable ProAuto a value of "high," if it was above 0.12 (12 percent of the expendable income spent on automotive items) and "low," otherwise. The majority of cases were "low." Figure 9.1 gives the R screen for linking the training file ExpenditureAutoTrainBinary.csv.

Figure 9.2 displays the R correlation graphic, indicating a strong positive relationship between the expenditures on automotive items and driver's license, as well as strong negative relationships between the automotive expenditures and income and age.

Credit cards and churn have a notable relationship, indicating that they might contain some overlapping information, as do driver's license and age.

To run correlation over all variables, you need to make AutoCat an Input and re-execute the data. This yields the correlation graphic shown in Figure 9.2. The strongest correlations with AutoCat are Income and Age, with DrivLic also appearing to have something to contribute. However,

Table 9.1 ExpenditureAutoNewBinary.csv

Age	Gender	Marital	Dependents	Income	YrJob	YrTown	YrEd	DrivLic	OwnHome	CredC	Churn	AutoBin
22	0	0	0	18	0	3	16	1	0	4	0	?
24	1	1	1	21	1	1	12	1	0	3	1	?
26	0	0.5	3	25	5	3	16	1	1	6	0	?
27	1	1	2	24	2	2	14	1	0	2	0	?
29	0	0	0	27	4	4	11	1	0	3	1	?
31	1	0	0	28	0	3	12	1	0	4	0	?
33	0	1	1	29	3	16	14	1	1	2	1	?
33	1	0.5	0	31	2	33	18	0	0	3	0	?
34	0	1	3	44	8	24	16	1	1	6	1	?
36	1	0	0	27	12	12	14	1	0	1	0	?
37	0	0	0	35	19	5	12	1	0	2	0	?
39	1	1	2	52	2	2	18	1	1	5	1	?
41	0	0.5	0	105	16	4	16	1	1	3	0	?
42	1	1	3	70	15	14	12	1	1	4	0	?
44	0	0	0	66	12	8	16	1	0	3	1	?
47	1	1	1	44	6	6	12	1	0	3	1	?
52	0	0.5	0	65	20	52	12	1	1	2	0	?
55	1	1	0	72	21	22	18	1	1	2	1	?
56	0	1	0	87	16	3	12	1	1	1	0	?
66	1	0	0	55	0	18	12	0	1	1	0	?

Figure 9.1 Data input

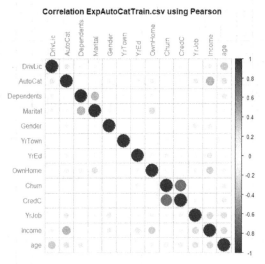

Figure 9.2 Rattle correlation graphic

Age and DrivLic have nearly as strong a correlation with Income as does with AutoCat, so we might leave it out and prune our model to include only Income as an independent variable.

Logistic Regression

The logistic regression model with all the available independent variables is shown in Figure 9.3.

R reports a Pseudo R-squared for logistic regression models. In this case, it was 0.776 for the model using all independent variables.

The pruned model using only Income and Drivers License is shown in Figure 9.4. It has a pseudo R-square of 0.774, nearly as strong as the model in Figure 9.3 which had 12 independent variables. We expect this model to be much stabler, and to predict, we only need values for income and driver's license.

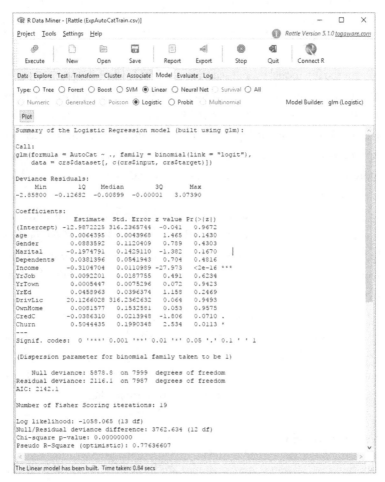

Figure 9.3 Rattle logistic regression model for auto expenditures

```
Coefficients:
              Estimate Std. Error z value Pr(>|z|)
(Intercept) -12.37669  311.98245  -0.040    0.968
Income       -0.30259    0.01036 -29.197   <2e-16 ***
DrivLic      20.09847  311.98248   0.064    0.949
```

Figure 9.4 Pruned Regression Model

We can test both models with a test set of 2000 observations.

Table 9.2 Coincidence matrix for full and pruned logistic regression models

FULL	Full 0	Full 1	Total		PRUNED	Pru 0	Pru 1	Total
Actual 0	1709	52	1761		Actual 0	1710	51	1761
Actual 1	66	173	239		Actual 1	62	177	239
	1775	225	2000			1772	228	2000

For the full model overall accuracy was 0.941, while the pruned model had 0.943. In predicting low automotive expenditure, the full model was 0.970 accurate over the test set (1709/1761), while the pruned model was 0.971. In predicting high automotive expenditure, the full model was 0.724 accurate, and the pruned model 0.741. Thus the pruned model was more accurate (slightly) on all three metrics, and provides a much stabler predictive model.

Evaluate tab. Note that you need to click on the *Score* button, link the *CSV File* (ExpenditureAutoNewBin.csv), and select the *Class* button because this data has a categorical output (if you were running a linear regression on numerical data, you would select the *Probability* button, which would provide you with the logistic function between 0 and 1 – Rattle uses a default cutoff of 0.5).

This creates an Excel-readable file that can be stored on your hard drive. Table 9.3 shows the inputs used by the logistic regression and the output in terms of classification. The full model provided the same classification predictions, with very similar probability predictions.

Neural Networks

The training, test, and new case files are loaded the same as with the logistic regression section. All Figure 9.5 shows is clicking on the *Neural Net* button.

Table 9.3 *Logistic regression application*

NewCase	Marital	Income	DrivLic	Class
1	0	18	1	High
2	1	21	1	High
3	0.5	25	1	Low
4	1	24	1	High
5	0	27	1	Low
6	0	28	1	Low
7	1	29	1	Low
8	0.5	31	0	Low
9	1	44	1	Low
10	0	27	1	Low
11	0	35	1	Low
12	1	52	1	Low
13	0.5	105	1	Low
14	1	70	1	Low
15	0	66	1	Low
16	1	44	1	Low
17	0.5	65	1	Low
18	1	72	1	Low
19	1	87	1	Low
20	0	55	0	Low

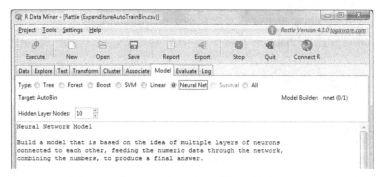

Figure 9.5 *Running neural network model*

The neural network model is run by clicking on *Execute*. The default model used 10 hidden layers, yielding a degenerate model calling all test cases low. Raising the hidden node level to 25 gave a more useful model.

Table 9.4 Neural network model coincidence matrix

	Full 0	Full 1	Total
Actual high	1713	48	1761
Actual low	66	173	239
	1779	221	2000

The resulting coincidence matrix is shown in Table 9.4.

This yields a correct classification rate of 0.943. High cases were correctly predicted 173/239, or 0.724, while low probability cases were correctly predicted 1,713/1,761, or 0.973. Application to the new cases resulted in every new case being predicted the same as with the logistic regression models.

Decision Tree

The inputs are the same as with the other models. The decision tree is reported in Figure 9.6.

The asterisks in Figure 9.6 indicate the seven rules obtained. Figure 9.7 shows the R graphic of this tree obtained by selecting the *Draw* button.

Note that only Income and DrivLic were used, despite all variables selected as being available in the training set. The coincidence matrix is given in Table 9.5.

This yields a correct classification rate of 0.943. The correct prediction of high probability cases was 0.707 while the correct prediction of low probability cases was 0.974. The application to the new cases resulted in predicting cases 1 through 4 as high, the rest low.

Comparison

Table 9.6 compares these models.

All three models had similar accuracies, on all three dimensions (although the decision tree was better at predicting high expenditure, and correspondingly lower at predicting low expenditure). The neural network didn't predict any high expenditure cases, but it was the least accurate at doing that in the test case. The decision tree model predicted

```
R Data Miner - [Rattle (ExpAutoCatTrain.csv)]                              —    □    ×
Project  Tools  Settings  Help                              Rattle Version 5.1.0 togaware.com

   Execute   New    Open   Save   Report   Export   Stop   Quit   Connect R

Data  Explore  Test  Transform  Cluster  Associate  Model  Evaluate  Log

Type: ● Tree ○ Forest ○ Boost ○ SVM ○ Linear ○ Neural Net ○ Survival ○ All

Target: AutoCat  Algorithm: ● Traditional ○ Conditional           Model Builder: rpart

Min Split:  20        Max Depth:  3        Priors:                   □ Include Missing

Min Bucket:  7        Complexity:  0.0100   Loss Matrix:              Rules  Draw

Summary of the Decision Tree model for Classification (built using 'rpart'):

n= 8000

node), split, n, loss, yval, (yprob)
      * denotes terminal node

 1) root 8000 962 0 (0.879750000 0.120250000)
   2) Income>=32.0755 6130   41 0 (0.993311582 0.006688418) *
   3) Income< 32.0755 1870  921 0 (0.507486631 0.492513369)
     6) Income>=21.121 1341 485 0 (0.638329605 0.361670395)
      12) DrivLic< 0.5 150    0 0 (1.000000000 0.000000000) *
      13) DrivLic>=0.5 1191 485 0 (0.592779177 0.407220823)
        26) Income>=27.0645 622 169 0 (0.728295820 0.271704180) *
        27) Income< 27.0645 569 253 1 (0.444639719 0.555360281)
          54) Income>=24.727 263 125 0 (0.524714829 0.475285171) *
          55) Income< 24.727 306 115 1 (0.375816993 0.624183007) *
     7) Income< 21.121 529   93 1 (0.175803403 0.824196597)
      14) DrivLic< 0.5 56     0 0 (1.000000000 0.000000000) *
      15) DrivLic>=0.5 473   37 1 (0.078224101 0.921775899) *
```

Figure 9.6 Decision tree model

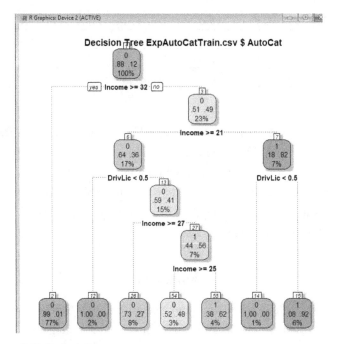

Figure 9.7 R decision tree

Table 9.5 Decision tree model coincidence matrix

DT	Full 0	Full 1	Total
Actual 0	1715	46	1761
Actual 1	70	169	239
	1785	215	2000

Table 9.6 Model comparisons in predicting auto expenditures

	Logistic regression	Neural network	Decision tree
Overall accuracy	0.943	0.943	0.943
High accuracy	0.741	0.724	0.707
Low accuracy	0.971	0.973	0.974
Case 1	High	High	High
Case 2	High	High	High
Case 3	Low	High	High
Case 4	High	High	High
Case 5	Low	Low	Low
Case 6	Low	Low	Low
Case 7	Low	Low	Low
Case 8	Low	Low	Low
Case 9	Low	Low	Low
Case 10	Low	Low	High

more high cases. These results are typical and to be expected—different models will yield different results, and these relative advantages are liable to change with new data. That is why automated systems applied to big data should probably utilize all three types of models. Data scientists need to focus attention on refining the parameters in each model type, seeking better fits for specific applications.

Summary

We have concluded this short book demonstrating R (Rattle) computations for the basic classification algorithms in data mining on a slightly larger dataset than we have used in prior chapters. The advent of big data has led to an environment where billions of records are possible. This book has not demonstrated that scope by any means, but it has demonstrated the small-scale version of the basic algorithms. The intent is to make data mining less of a black-box exercise, thus hopefully enabling users to be more intelligent in their application of data mining.

We have demonstrated three open source software products in earlier chapters of the book. KNIME has a very interesting GUI, demonstrating the data mining process in an object-oriented format. But, it is a little more involved for the user. WEKA is a very good tool, especially for users who want to compare different algorithms within each category. However, it is problematic in dealing with test files and new case files (it can work, it just doesn't always). Thus, R is the recommended software. R is widely used in industry and has all of the benefits of open source software (many eyes are monitoring it, leading to fewer bugs; it is free; it is scalable). Further, the R system enables widespread data manipulation and management.

Notes

Chapter 1

1. Davenport (2014).
2. Mayer–Schonberger and Cukier (2013).
3. Cukier and Mayer–Schoenberger (2013).
4. Sathi (2012).
5. Szkolar (2013).
6. Evans (2015).

Chapter 2

1. Ponduri and Bala (2014).
2. Snyder (2014).
3. Bholat (2015).
4. Donovan (2015).
5. Canzian and van der Schaar (2015).
6. Olson and Chae (2012).
7. Sung, Chang, and Lee (1999).

Chapter 4

1. Olson, Delen, and Meng (2012).

Chapter 6

1. Dielman (2001).

Chapter 7

1. Churchland (1997).
2. Kohonen (1988).

References

Bholat, D. 2015. "Big Data and Central Banks." *Bank of England Quarterly Bulletin* 55, no. 1, pp. 86–93.

Canzian, L., and M. van der Schaar. 2015. "Real-Time Stream Mining: Online Knowledge Extraction Using Classifier Networks." *IEEE Network* 29, no. 5, pp. 10–16.

Churchland, P. 1997. *Matter and Consciousness,* 154. 8th printing, Cambridge, MA: Bradford Books/The MIT Press.

Cukier, K.N., and V. Mayer-Schoenberger. May–June 2013. "The Rise of Big Data: How It's Changing the Way We Think About the World." In *The Fourth Industrial Revolution: A Davos Reader*, ed. G. Rose, Chapter 3 (from *Foreign Affairs*).

Davenport, T.H. 2014. *Big Data at Work*. Boston, MA: Harvard Business Review Press.

Dielman, T. 2001. *Applied Regression Analysis for Business and Economics,* 563–70. 3rd ed. Duxbury.

Donovan, K. 2015. "Mining (and Minding) the Data." *Best's Review*, p. 46.

Evans, M. 2015. "Healthcare Data Mining." *Modern Healthcare* 45, no. 39, p. 24.

Kohonen, T. 1988. *"Self-Organization and Associative Memory."* New York: Springer.

Mayer-Schonberger, V., and K. Cukier. 2013. *Big Data: A Revolution that Will Transform How We Live, Work, and Think*. New York: Houghton Mifflin Harcourt.

Olson, D.L., and B. Chae. 2012. "Direct Marketing Decision Support Through Predictive Customer Response Modeling." *Decision Support Systems* 54, no. 1, pp. 443–51.

Olson, D.L., D. Delen, and Y. Meng. 2012. "Comparative Analysis of Data Mining Methods for Bankruptcy Prediction." *Decision Support Systems* 52, pp. 464–73.

Ponduri, S.B., and E.S. Bala. 2014. "Role of Information Technology in Effective Implementation of Customer Relationship Management." *Journal of Marketing and Communication* 9, no. 3, pp. 50–55.

Sathi, A. 2012. *Big Data Analytics: Disruptive Technologies for Changing the Game*. Boise, ID: MC Press. Snyder, N. 2014. "Mining Data to Make Money." *Bank Director* 24, no. 3, pp. 27–28.

Snyder, N. 2014. "Mining Data to Make Money." *Bank Director* 24, no. 3, pp. 27–28.

Sung, T.K., N. Chang, and G. Lee. 1999. "Dynamics of Modeling in Data Mining: Interpretive Approach to Bankruptcy Prediction." *Journal of Management Information Systems* 16, no. 1, pp. 63–85.

Szkolar, D. January 24, 2013. "Data Mining in Obama's 2012 victory." *Information Space.* infospace.ischool.syr.edu/2013/01/24/

Index

OTHER TITLES IN OUR BIG DATA AND BUSINESS ANALYTICS COLLECTION

Mark Ferguson, University of South Carolina, Editor

- *Business Intelligence and Data Mining* by Anil Maheshwari
- *Data Mining Models* by David L. Olson
- *Big Data War: How to Survive Global Big Data Competition* by Patrick Park
- *Analytics Boot Camp: Basic Analytics for Business Students and Professionals* by Linda Herkenhoff and John Fogli

FORTHCOMING TITLES FOR THIS COLLECTION

- *Predictive Analytics: An Introduction to Big Data, Data Mining, and Text Mining* by Barry Keating
- *Business Location Analytics: The Research and Marketing Strategic Advantage* by David Z. Beitz
- *Business Analytics: A Data-Driven Decision Making Approach for Business* by Amar Sahay

Announcing the Business Expert Press Digital Library

Concise e-books business students need for classroom and research

This book can also be purchased in an e-book collection by your library as

- a one-time purchase,
- that is owned forever,
- allows for simultaneous readers,
- has no restrictions on printing, and
- can be downloaded as PDFs from within the library community.

Our digital library collections are a great solution to beat the rising cost of textbooks. E-books can be loaded into their course management systems or onto students' e-book readers. The **Business Expert Press** digital libraries are very affordable, with no obligation to buy in future years. For more information, please visit **www.businessexpertpress.com/librarians**. To set up a trial in the United States, please email **sales@businessexpertpress.com**.